THE VEGETARIAN BARBECUE

A Guide to Gourmet Eating Outdoors

by

DAVID ENO

Illustrated by Kim Blundell

A THORSONS WHOLEFOOD COOKBOOK

THORSONS PUBLISHERS LIMITED
Wellingborough, Northamptonshire

First published June 1984
Second Impression June 1985
Third Impression May 1986

British Library Cataloguing in Publication Data

Eno, David
    The vegetarian barbecue.
    1. Vegetarian cookery.   2. Barbecue cookery
    I. Title
    641.7'6   TX837

ISBN 0-7225-0792-5

Printed in Great Britain by
Richard Clay (The Chaucer Press) Ltd,
Bungay, Suffolk

CONTENTS

INTRODUCTION

Although the conventional barbecue meal is centred around meat there is no need for vegetarians to forgo the social and gastronomic pleasures of eating barbecued food. In this book you will find a whole range of alternatives which have been especially created or adapted for vegetarian barbecue cooking.

Barbecues are one of the easiest and most relaxing ways of entertaining and make much more of an 'event' than an ordinary meal. They are popular with adults and children alike and are ideal for parties and celebrations. Their use for normal family meals should not be neglected and, in the warmer months, a barbecue lunch or evening meal out in the fresh air can be very enjoyable. Whatever the event, the cook is not banished to the kitchen while the meal is being prepared. In fact, family or guests will probably be eager to lend a hand.

Don't be put off by the expensive barbecues displayed in shops and garden centres. If you find you are regularly eating barbecue meals you may like to splash out on one of these, but to begin with you can manage with a bag of charcoal and a few bricks, or one of the very cheap Japanese 'hibachi'-type barbecues. The essence of barbecue cookery is simplicity and, to my mind, this is the way it should be kept. Use the best of fresh and wholesome ingredients and, as with all cookery books, do not feel you have to follow the recipes to the letter. Use them as a basis for your own ideas.

Choosing Barbecue Equipment

As you will not be cooking meat the more complicated and expensive spit-type barbecues will be unnecessary, in fact you can go a long way with something quite basic. If you are really keen on barbecue cooking you may wish to build a permanent barbecue in your garden and this is discussed later. Most people start by buying one of the portable or table-top barbecues which, even if later you move on to something larger, is a good way to begin and is always useful for picnics, beach parties or camping, or as an additional unit if you are catering for large numbers.

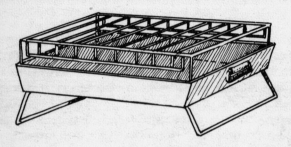

Figure 1.   Portable barbecue.

Portable barbecues: Camping shops and garden centres usually have a selection of barbecues which can be folded and transported easily. These will fit into a compact space in the boot of a car, although to avoid spreading ash and grease it's best to store them in a heavy duty plastic sack.

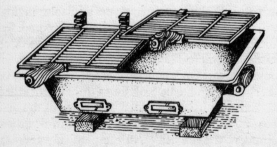

Figure 2.   Table-top barbecue.

Table-top barbecues: These are among the smallest and cheapest and are ideal if you are restricted to a small space in which to have your barbecue. Although table-top and some portable models come without a stand you can always make your own if necessary. Cooking is much easier if it can be done at normal table-top height. One rather clever solution shown me by a friend is to use the folding tubular legs from a child's high chair. For the handyman or woman a visit to the local scrapyard or dump will always provide some useful materials.

Figure 3. Free-standing types of barbecue.

Free-standing barbecues: There are many types available ranging from simple units to the highly sophisticated which incorporate features such as adjustable grills, warming ovens, hoods, thermometers, electric lighters, adjustable dampers, double fireboxes, tool racks, and, of course, various spits, some motor driven, which are used for cooking meat. The larger units tend to be built into a trolley with wheels for easy mobility and may have the added advantage of drawers and storage cupboards. The more you pay the more control you get over the cooking process; the fire can be lit more quickly and adjusted more precisely; the grill can be set in a number of positions to get the desired heat.

Making Your Own Simple Barbecue

You don't need to be proficient at bricklaying or metalwork to make your own barbecue. Here are some ways of improvising a simple barbecue with little or no handiwork at all.

Figure 4.   Cast iron skillet.

Cast Iron Skillet: If you have a thick cast iron skillet, place it on a couple of bricks, line it with foil and put a layer of gravel in the bottom, one to two inches (2.5 to 5cm) deep. Make the fire on top of this and either skewer food or use a wire rack for the grill, supported on more bricks if necessary. Any similar thick metal container can be used — but nothing precious!

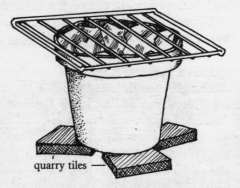

Figure 5.   Flowerpot barbecue.

Flowerpot Barbecue: A large clay flowerpot makes an effective barbeque. It should be completely lined with thick aluminium foil and have a generous layer of gravel at the bottom. To provide a draught make sure to poke a hole through the foil where the pot drainage hole is, and support the pot on a few bricks or tiles to allow the air to flow underneath. To avoid the pot cracking the fire should be started slowly and the heat increased gradually. On no account use when damp or douse with water after use.

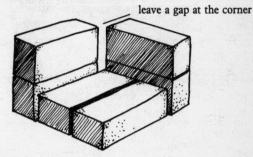

leave a gap at the corner

Figure 6.   Partly built loose brick barbecue.

Loose Brick Barbecue: Loose bricks can be used to make a temporary barbecue. For the simplest configuration, ten bricks are required. Place two bricks together to form the base and make the four walls by building each with two bricks one on top of the other. Leave a slight gap at each corner for ventilation. To avoid damage to grass build on a paving slab, path or patio.

Figure 7.   Log barbecue.

Log Barbecue: The barbecue fire can be contained by a circle of thick logs stood on end. These will also provide a base for the grill and a place to put utensils and keep food warm. As the logs slowly burn they will impart their own smoky taste to the food.

More Ambitious Home-Made Barbecues

Anyone proficient in metalwork will be able to use, or elaborate on, the ideas below to produce an effective barbecue. If you lack the expertise but do have a particular idea in mind you could try a blacksmith who will probably find it an interesting challenge, but enquire first about the cost.

Oil Drum Barbecues: Large oil drums can be used in several ways but will require heavy cutting tools and possibly the use of a welder. One method is to cut the drum in half lengthways, which will make a

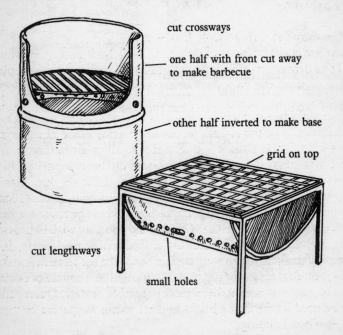

Figure 8.   Oil drum barbecues.

large barbecue suitable for fêtes and public events. Legs of round or square section tubular steel will be needed for this type.

If the drum is cut in half crossways one half can be inverted and used as a base while the other is shaped as illustrated to make the barbecue. Wire mesh can be used above and below the fire, and will need to be removable so that the ashes can be cleaned out. Although the draught can be provided by holes punched in the bottom and sides, a more controlled airflow is preferable and could be achieved by the shutter arrangement illustrated.

Sheet Metal Barbecues: Depending on the equipment you have available there are many ways of making barbecues out of sheet metal ranging from a simple tray or box through to elaborate shapes which require complicated cutting and welding. Have a look at some of the commercial designs and see if you think any would be effective and easy to make.

A Permanent Brick-Built Barbecue

There are countless ways of designing brick-built barbecues which will be a permanent garden feature. You may wish to follow the plan below or work out your own arrangement on paper or with loose bricks.

The main requirement is for a structure which will support two metal grids. The fire is built on the lower grid, which must have a space below it open on at least one side to allow air to flow in and ashes to be scraped out. The food is placed on the upper grid, which should be at least four inches (10cm) above the lower one. Ideally you could provide for several positions between four inches (10cm) and one foot (30cm). The top of the barbecue should be at a convenient working height, say 30 inches (75cm), and you may wish to provide extra shelves or ledges for utensils or for keeping food warm. It is especially useful to have a work surface beside the barbecue as it makes life a great deal easier for the cook. This could be a couple of paving slabs or, more ornamentally, a piece of marble or slate. Quarry tiles can be used for surfacing bricks and are useful as spacers between bricks when building.

Taking the barbecue to its ultimate conclusion, you could build a complete outdoor kitchen as an extension to your house or summerhouse with one or more sides open onto the garden and generous working surfaces and storage.

The siting of a permanent barbecue needs careful thought. While it should be convenient to the kitchen and patio or seating area, consider any possible fire hazards such as garden sheds, wooden fences or buildings. Smoke may cause annoyance to neighbours but careful siting could help to avoid or, at least reduce, this. To keep smoke away from the eating area you may like to consider building a short chimney which will also provide shelter and conserve much of the heat, preventing the food from being cooled by draughts.

The barbecue to be described has three brick walls with the fourth side open. This opening should be positioned so that it catches the prevailing wind. In practice you will not want to use the barbecue when it is very windy but being able to catch even a slight breeze will be an advantage.

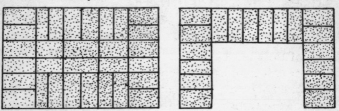

first layer   third and fifth layer

second and fourth layer   front view

space for fire

space for ashes   grate
cooking grid ⎱ 2 grids

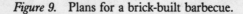

Figure 9. Plans for a brick-built barbecue.

Approximately one and a half hundredweights (dry weight) of cement and sand will be required and, to prevent undue stress and cracking, a fairly thin mix is best, about five parts sand to one of cement. A masonry sawing disc (and suitable dust mask) is very useful for cutting and shaping bricks and quarry tiles.

Prepare a foundation by digging out a four by two-and-a-half foot (1.2m × 75cm) rectangle of soil to a depth of six inches (15cm). Fill with hardcore and ram down well, adding more until the surrounding ground level is reached.

Prepare a layer of cement and bed in the first layer of bricks as illustrated. Spread more cement to accommodate the second layer, and so on, until complete. In very hot weather protect from rapid drying by covering with damp sacking. Cover also to protect from frost, but do not work in freezing cold weather. Leave for at least a week before use so that the cement has a chance to dry out properly.

The metal grids can be made from metal door scrapers or may be bought from a blacksmith or metal workshop. To make a long lasting grid for the fire ⅜ inch (1cm) metal bars welded to a frame at ½ inch (1.5cm) intervals are the ideal solution.

Choice of Fuel

The choice of fuel for barbecue cooking is between wood, charcoal and charcoal briquettes. Wood, although easy to light, takes longer to burn down to a satisfactory bed of coals and will need to be started at least an hour and a half before cooking time.

Dry, slow-burning hardwoods such as oak, apple, ash, walnut, beech and sycamore make the best cooking fires. Avoid soft resinous woods such as larch or spruce as they make a lot of pungent smoke which tends to discolour the food and give it an unpleasant taste. The smoke from a wood fire may cause problems, although this should have subsided before any serious cooking begins.

For a fast, hot and clean fire it is far better to use charcoal or briquettes. Briquettes are made from ground charcoal moulded into uniform pieces and tend to burn for longer, with a more uniform heat than ordinary charcoal. They do cost more, however, and for all normal circumstances I find ordinary charcoal quite satisfactory.

To Make Your Own Charcoal

If you have a plentiful supply of dry hardwood you can make your own charcoal very easily. Get a good fire going then pile as much wood on as possible to form a neat pyramid so that all the flames are covered. Next cover the fire completely with turves or earth. The fire will burn slowly for many hours (making a lot of smoke) and when it eventually goes out you should have a good supply of charcoal. If you live near the sea you may be able to go beachcombing for suitable pieces of wood.

Building and Lighting the Fire

The first step in successful barbecuing is to get a good fire going well in advance of the time you need to start cooking. The *minimum* time it takes to start a barbecue is half an hour, while to be on the safe side you should allow three-quarters to one hour.

It is essential to have a strong enough draught passing through the coals. One way of improving this, particularly with solid bottomed or home-made barbecues where the bottom draught is lacking, is to begin by making a layer of gravel chippings. This not only improves the draught but helps retain the heat and makes it more uniform. It also protects the bottom of your barbecue from burning through, which tends to happen with barbecues made of thin sheet steel. The ashes can be separated from the gravel after use with a garden sieve and the gravel re-used again and again. Alternatively, aluminium foil can be used, which also protects to some extent and, if used with the shiny side uppermost, reflects the heat back. Both gravel and foil make it easier to clean out the barbecue after use.

The best method of lighting a barbecue is a subject of great controversy between enthusiasts. Some will tell you to start the fire with small kindling sticks, others swear by fire lighting blocks or methylated spirits. Failing anything else I occasionally use a gas blowtorch, but by far the quickest and easiest method is to use either the barbecue lighting fluid sold in plastic bottles, or less expensively, plain paraffin. To use either of these, tip in enough charcoal to make a heap, about nine inches (25cm) in diameter and six inches (15cm) high, in the centre of the barbecue. Sprinkle with lighting fluid and leave for a few minutes to soak in. Ignite, then leave for twenty minutes.

An old washing-up liquid bottle is a good container for paraffin as it allows only a small, measured dose to be sprinkled over the coals. When travelling make sure that lighting fluids are stored in secure containers and stowed safely. Paraffin is smelly, so be careful not to spill it all over the place. Then, provided the fire is allowed to get hot enough to burn away the last traces before cooking commences, it will not taint the food.

If using firelighters, two or three should be sufficient. They must be broken into several smaller pieces and mixed with the charcoal. Light them, then pile on more charcoal and leave. The other methods seem very slow compared to these, which usually produce a fire hot enough for cooking in 20 to 30 minutes.

At this stage a word of caution: lighting fluid or paraffin poured onto *cold* charcoal is relatively safe for use by responsible adults. Never, *never* use petrol or other inflammable liquids, and do not pour paraffin onto a hot fire as it can flare up and cause serious burns.

Whatever method you choose for lighting, it helps to make a pile of charcoal in the centre of the barbecue. For really fast lighting you can also use a chimney which increases the draught through the charcoal and gets you off to a roaring start in no time. To make a chimney take the largest and tallest food tin you can find (the sort that fruit juice sometimes comes in is ideal) and remove top and bottom with a tin opener. Drill or punch with a series of holes all the way around one end; just above the rim. To start the fire make a shallow

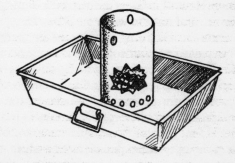

Figure 10. Home-made chimney to speed up lighting.

layer of charcoal and place the chimney on top. Pour more charcoal into the chimney then light.

Various electric starters are available which also ensure a fast and trouble free start for your barbecue, although you will have to pay for this extra convenience. The electric paint strippers which have recently come onto the market can also be used and will very quickly produce a good fire.

The fire is ready for cooking when the charcoal has warmed to a red glow and is covered with a thin layer of white ash. By this stage the smoke will have died down. This may be difficult to see on a bright day. If you can hold the palm of your hand near the grill for more than three seconds then the fire is not hot enough, but if its too hot to stand for this time then the fire is probably ready for cooking.

Regulating the Fire
Successful cooking can only take place on the radiant heat from glowing coals — not the scorching heat of flames. The idea is to use your skill and judgement to cook the food evenly throughout rather than burning the outside and leaving the centre uncooked. Apart from raising or lowering the grill it is possible to make some adjustment to the heat of the fire. Stirring the coals to remove ash will increase the heat, whilst moving the coals out from the centre of the fire will decrease it. A light sprinkling of water is another way of quickly reducing the heat. If you will be needing the fire for a while longer you can also reduce the heat by sprinkling on fresh charcoal. If you wish to add more charcoal *without* reducing the heat, add it around the edge of the fire and leave to warm for fifteen to twenty minutes then rake it into the centre of the fire where it should ignite immediately. Regulating the air supply will also make the fire burn more or less fiercely. Keep some water handy just in case of accidents. A watering can could be very useful in an emergency.

To reduce the amount of smoke generated by the fire use the minimum amount of fat or oil necessary and try to prevent it from dripping into the fire. It helps to make as much use of aluminium foil as possible, although aromatic smoke has the advantage of adding flavour to the food. Woods which burn aromatically, such as apple or pear, can be added as chips. You could also try sprinkling the fire with rosemary, thyme, basil, bay or garlic cloves.

Utensils and Accessories

A good pair of **tongs** are indispensible for moving about the hot coals and manipulating the food. A sturdy long-handled pair will serve you best. Next in usefulness comes a **long-handled fork**. A **wok** with lid is the ideal type of pan to use on a barbecue for all types of cooking. Thick **aluminium foil** is also indispensable for the vegetarian barbecue as vegetables need to retain their moisture for successful cooking and do not respond in the same way as meat to cooking by radiant heat. **Brushes** are needed for basting food while it is cooking, preferably the bristle type rather than nylon which melts easily.

To keep the fire in order a **poker** is useful and for maintaining a good draught an **ash scraper** as illustrated would be useful. After use, a thorough brushing with a stiff **wire brush** is all that's needed to keep your barbecue in good and clean condition. **Kebab skewers**

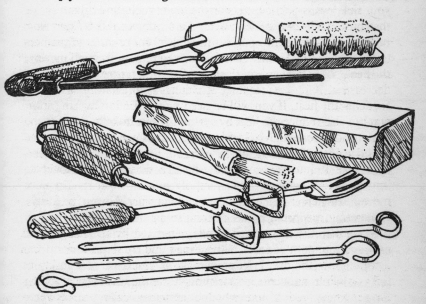

Figure 11. Accessories.

do not have to skewer meat — they can be used to cook all manner of vegetable delights. A pair of **oven gloves** are also a good idea especially for removing foil from cooked food. A **trolley** or **table** standing near the grill with everything to hand will make life a lot simpler for the cook.

Wooden bowls, boards and **plates** are particularly good for serving food out of doors as they are unbreakable and do not cool the food unduly. Never soak wood ware. Simply wipe clean with a damp cloth and rub in a little olive oil to seal the wood. After a while they develop a rich and beautiful patina. Plastic utensils have the same advantages but are less appealing to use and deteriorate more rapidly, especially around a hot fire.

Herbs and Seasonings

Use plenty of herbs and seasonings to complement the natural taste of barbecued food, but be careful not to smother it by over-seasoning. Mushrooms are complemented by basil, bay, chervil, chives, dill, garlic, marjoram, parsley, rosemary, sage, tarragon and thyme, while potatoes and rice are good with basil, chervil, chives, dill, lemon balm, marjoram, mint, parsley and summer savory. For other vegetables try bay, chives, dill, fennel, garlic, lemon balm, lovage, mint, parsley, rosemary, salad burnet, sorrel, summer savory, tarragon and thyme.

For seasoning I prefer sea salt, which has a more natural taste than ordinary salt and contains many trace elements often missing from heavily processed foods. Each is important in its own way for the correct functioning of the body. Celery salt is a useful seasoning as it adds flavour as well as salt. Garlic salt is another alternative and can be bought or made by grinding sliced garlic and sea salt together in a mortar and pestle or liquidizer. Dry the mixture in a warm place and afterwards grind again to reduce it to a powder. Always use freshly ground black peppercorns rather than pre-ground pepper which tends to be hot without any flavour. Chilli is a very useful flavouring which derives from chilli peppers, part of the same family as the familiar green or red pepper. Chilli powder should be used very carefully as it can be extremely pungent, although strength varies enormously. Take the time to add in very small amounts, tasting in between. Tabasco sauce is another, and slightly safer, way of adding hot chilli flavouring and can be added a few drops at a time. *Holbrook's* Worcester sauce is another useful ready made flavouring and is useful if you decide that what you are cooking is a little too bland.

Soya sauce is often used to flavour rice dishes, although it has many other uses. The cheap varieties are coloured with caramel and are rather salty without having much flavour. Tamari soya sauce is made from fermented soya beans and is far superior, so try to get this if you can.

All recipes serve four, unless stated otherwise.

1.

BURGERS AND SAUSAGES

In the traditional barbecue, burgers and sausages form a large part of the menu. These pleasures need not be denied the vegetarian as there are many meatless substitutes which can be bought or made at home. Although some purists may dismiss these on the basis that they are a meat imitation, my own feeling is that burgers and sausages have the least 'meaty' characteristics of any of the carnivorous foods and that they provide a substitute not for meat itself but for a texture which can be lacking in vegetarian food.

Frozen vegetarian burgers are now widely available and are very convenient, although I personally prefer some of the other dry mixes such as *Sosmix*, which I think have a better flavour and texture and which can be modified during the mixing. I like to add herbs, fried onions, freshly ground black pepper and sometimes a little crushed garlic to improve the flavour.

Serving Suggestions
As with most vegetarian foods, every part of the traditional hamburger can be improved upon to such an extent that even hardened meat eaters will actually prefer them. For a start, wholemeal rolls have a far more interesting flavour and texture. Some very good wholemeal rolls are available these days, and most bakeries have a selection. I like particularly the 'Turkestan' rolls which have a moist, grainy texture and are topped with crunchy cracked wheat and sesame seeds. If you prefer to make your own rolls there is a recipe on page 34.

Home made or good quality bought relishes and chutneys can add the finishing touch to a really succulent barbecue hamburger. Most supermarkets now carry a range of relishes including barbecue relish, tomato, onion, cucumber, sweetcorn and others.

Burger and Sausage Mixes

The recipes which follow will all need preparation beforehand but, once formed into burgers or sausages, they freeze well, which can be a useful time saver. Just lay them out on trays until frozen and, when hard, store in sealed bags. Allow not less than 15 minutes to defrost before cooking on the grill over hot charcoal. Turn several times until done.

For sausages, a uniform mixture is essential, so make sure that beans are well mashed or nuts, if used, are very finely chopped. Breadcrumbs should be minced or liquidized. Use plenty of seasoning including freshly ground black pepper and herbs such as thyme and sage. Although the mixture can be rolled into shape, an icing bag without the nozzle produces a better result.

LENTIL OR BEAN BURGER MIX

Imperial (Metric)	American
½ lb (225g) red lentils	1 cupful red lentils
2 onions, chopped	2 onions, chopped
1 clove garlic	1 clove garlic
2 tablespoonsful vegetable oil	2 tablespoonsful vegetable oil
2 cupsful wholemeal breadcrumbs	2½ cupsful wholewheat breadcrumbs
1 tablespoonful chopped parsley	1 tablespoonful chopped parsley
1 teaspoonful chopped sage	1 teaspoonful chopped sage
1 teaspoonful chopped thyme	1 teaspoonful chopped thyme
Sea salt and freshly ground black pepper	Sea salt and freshly ground black pepper
2 eggs	2 eggs
4 oz (115g) grated Cheddar cheese	1 cupful grated Cheddar cheese

1. Cook the lentils in three times their own volume of water, which should take about 15 minutes.

2. Fry the chopped onion and garlic in the oil and, when cooked,

add to the breadcrumbs in a mixing bowl.

3. Add the chopped herbs, salt and pepper, then mix.

4. Finally add the eggs, the grated cheese and the cooked lentils and mix thoroughly. If the mixture will not form into burgers add a few more breadcrumbs to dry it a little.

Note: Any type of cooked bean may be substituted for the lentils.

BARBECUE BEAN BURGER MIX

Imperial (Metric)	American
½ lb (225g) soaked red kidney beans (*or* 1 tin red kidney beans)	1 cupful soaked red kidney beans (*or* 1 can red kidney beans)
2 large onions, chopped	2 large onions, chopped
1½ oz (40g) butter	3 tablespoonsful butter
4 tablespoonsful chopped parsley	4 tablespoonsful chopped parsley
2 oz (55g) wholemeal flour	½ cupful wholewheat flour
2 oz (55g) wholemeal breadcrumbs	1 cupful wholewheat breadcrumbs
1 tablespoonful soya sauce	1 tablespoonful soy sauce
1 tablespoonful tomato purée	1 tablespoonful tomato paste

1. Leave the beans to soak overnight.

2. Next day boil in a large pan with plenty of water (and no salt).

3. While the beans are cooking, sauté the onion in the butter until soft.

4. When the beans are cooked, which will take at least 30 minutes, strain in a colander then mash.

5. Stir in the cooked onions and the rest of the ingredients and leave to cool.

6. Roll out on a floured board and cut into rounds with a large tumbler or biscuit cutter to form into sausages.

7. Grill, basting with butter or oil, until crisp on both sides and serve.

VEGETABLE BURGER MIX

Imperial (Metric)	American
2 medium onions	2 medium onions
1 clove garlic	1 clove garlic
1 tablespoonful butter	1 tablespoonful butter
1 tablespoonful vegetable oil	1 tablespoonful vegetable oil
1 large aubergine	1 large eggplant
4 oz (115g) mushrooms	2 cupsful mushrooms
14 oz (400g) tin tomatoes	14 ounces can red tomatoes
1 teaspoonful chopped fresh thyme	1 teaspoonful chopped fresh thyme
Sea salt	Sea salt
Freshly ground black pepper	Freshly ground black pepper
4 oz (115g) red lentils	½ cupful red lentils
4 oz (115g) wholemeal breadcrumbs	1 cupful wholewheat breadcrumbs

1. Thinly slice the onion and garlic and sauté in the butter and oil until soft.

2. Chop the aubergine (eggplant) and mushrooms and add to the onion.

3. Add the tomatoes, herbs and seasonings and simmer gently for 15 minutes so that some of the juice evaporates.

4. In a separate pan cook the lentils for 15 minutes, by which time all the water should have been absorbed.

5. Stir in the lentils and breadcrumbs and leave to stand for 5 minutes.

6. Form into burgers and grill, basting with oil or butter, until nicely browned on both sides.

MUSHROOM BURGER MIX

Imperial (Metric)	American
2 medium onions	2 medium onions
1 green pepper	1 green pepper
1 oz (30g) butter	2½ tablespoonsful butter
½ lb (225g) mushrooms	4 cups mushrooms
4 oz (115g) wholemeal breadcrumbs	1 cupful wholewheat breadcrumbs
2 eggs	2 eggs
Sea salt	Sea salt
Freshly ground black pepper	Freshly ground black pepper
1 teaspoonful mixed herbs	1 teaspoonful mixed herbs

1. Chop the onion and green pepper finely and fry in the butter until soft.

2. Chop half of the mushrooms finely and fry with the pepper and onion for a minute or two.

3. Remove from the heat and add the breadcrumbs and the eggs.

4. Mix well and season to taste with sea salt, freshly ground pepper and herbs.

5. Form into burgers or sausages and grill.

6. Slice the remainder of the mushrooms and fry in butter until brown.

7. Serve the burgers topped with mushrooms on a plate or in a hamburger roll.

CHESTNUT BURGER MIX

Imperial (Metric)
2 cupsful chestnut purée
1 cupful wholemeal breadcrumbs
1 tablespoonful chopped thyme
½ tablespoonful chopped sage
Sea salt and freshly ground black
  pepper
1 medium onion, finely chopped
2 tablespoonsful vegetable oil
1 egg

American
2½ cupsful chestnut paste
1¼ cupsful wholewheat
  breadcrumbs
1 tablespoonful chopped thyme
½ tablespoonful chopped sage
Sea salt and freshly ground black
  pepper
1 medium onion, finely chopped
2 tablespoonsful vegetable oil
1 egg

1. Mash the chestnut purée with the breadcrumbs, chopped herbs and seasoning.

2. Fry the finely chopped onion in vegetable oil and add to the mixture.

3. Break in the egg and mix well.

4. Form into burgers or sausages on a floured board, brush with oil and grill.

PEANUT BURGER MIX

Imperial (Metric)	American
2 medium onions	2 medium onions
2 tablespoonsful vegetable oil	2 tablespoonsful vegetable oil
½ lb (225g) peanuts	1½ cupsful peanuts
1 cupful wholemeal breadcrumbs	1¼ cupsful wholewheat breadcrumbs
1 tablespoonful chopped parsley	1 tablespoonful chopped parsley
1 teaspoonful chopped thyme	1 teaspoonful chopped thyme
Sea salt and freshly ground black pepper	Sea salt and freshly ground black pepper
1 oz (30g) vegetable margarine	2½ tablespoonsful vegetable margarine
2 eggs	2 eggs
1 tablespoonful tomato purée	1 tablespoonful tomato paste

1. Chop the onions and fry in a little vegetable oil, but do not allow to brown.

2. Put the nuts through a mincer or liquidize briefly. The idea is to chop them into small pieces without reducing them to paste.

3. Add the nuts to the breadcrumbs in a mixing bowl and stir in the chopped herbs, salt and pepper. Now add the cooked onion and rub in the margarine.

4. Mix in the two eggs which should bind the ingredients and give a workable consistency. Add the tomato purée and a little water if necessary.

5. Form into burgers and grill until browned on both sides.

POTATO AND NUT BURGERS

Imperial (Metric)	American
½ lb (225g) potatoes	8 ounces potatoes
2 tablespoonsful butter	2 tablespoonsful butter
1 medium onion	1 medium onion
4 oz (115g) mushrooms	2 cupsful mushrooms
2 tablespoonsful vegetable oil	2 tablespoonsful vegetable oil
Sea salt	Sea salt
Freshly ground black pepper	Freshly ground black pepper
1 tablespoonful chopped parsley	1 tablespoonful chopped parsley
3 oz (85g) chopped almonds or other nuts	¾ cupful chopped almonds or other nuts

1. Peel and boil the potatoes and, when cooked, mash with the butter.

2. While the potato is cooking, slice the onions and mushrooms and sauté in the oil.

3. Season the mashed potato and stir in the parsley, cooked onion, mushroom and chopped nuts.

4. Form into burgers.

5. Brush with oil and grill.

RICE BURGERS

Imperial (Metric)	American
1 onion, chopped	1 onion, chopped
2 tablespoonsful oil	2 tablespoonsful oil
4 oz (115g) brown rice, cooked	½ cupful brown rice, cooked
2 tablespoonsful wholemeal breadcrumbs	2 tablespoonsful wholewheat breadcrumbs
2 oz (55g) Cheddar cheese, grated	½ cupful Cheddar cheese, grated
1 tablespoonful 81 per cent wholemeal self-raising flour	1 tablespoonful 81 per cent wholewheat self-raising flour
1 egg	1 egg
½ tablespoonful tomato purée	½ tablespoonful tomato paste
Sea salt	Sea salt
Freshly ground black pepper	Freshly ground black pepper

1. Fry the chopped onion in the oil.

2. When soft mix with the rice, breadcrumbs, grated cheese, flour, egg, tomato purée and seasonings to form a thick dough.

3. Form into burgers or sausages.

4. Brush with vegetable oil and grill or fry over charcoal, turning until both sides are golden brown.

5. Serve with wholemeal rolls and relish.

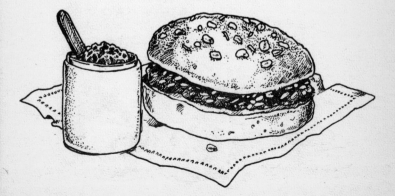

DRY MIX FOR BURGERS

Make up this dry mix and keep in a jar for immediate use at short notice.

Imperial (Metric)
2 oz (55g) hard vegetable fat
2 tablespoonsful freeze-dried chopped onions
½ lb (225g) peanuts
1 cupful wholemeal breadcrumbs
1 teaspoonful dried parsley
½ teaspoonful dried thyme
Sea salt and freshly ground black pepper

American
¼ cupful hard vegetable fat
2 tablespoonsful freeze-dried chopped onions
1½ cupsful peanuts
1¼ cupsful wholewheat breadcrumbs
1 teaspoonful dried parsley
½ teaspoonful dried thyme
Sea salt and freshly ground black pepper

1. Grate the vegetable fat with a medium grater.

2. Mix all the dry ingredients.

3. Stir the fat into the dry ingredients.

4. Store in an airtight jar in a cool place for up to 1 month.

5. To use, stir in enough water to form a stiff dough.

6. Form into burgers and grill.

CHEESE HAMBURGERS

Imperial (Metric)
1 small onion, chopped
1 oz (30g) butter
4 oz (115g) cheese, Cheddar or
  Gruyère
1 lb (455g) burger mix from any one
  of the previous recipes
1 teaspoonful English mustard
6 wholemeal hamburger rolls
Sea salt and freshly ground black
  pepper

American
1 small onion, chopped
2½ tablespoonsful butter
1 cupful cheese, Cheddar or Gruyère
1 pound burger mix from any one of
  the previous recipes
1 teaspoonful English mustard
6 wholewheat hamburger rolls
Sea salt and freshly ground black
  pepper

1. Sauté the onion in the butter until soft.

2. Grate the cheese into the burger mix and add the cooked onions and mustard.

3. Form into six burgers and cook over the grill for a few minutes each side until done.

4. Place in the split rolls and serve straight away with pickle or relish.

SALAD HAMBURGERS

Serve your burgers between wholemeal rolls with crisp lettuce, watercress and slices of tomato or any other salad ingredient which takes your fancy. Dress with your favourite relish or garlic mayonnaise.

CRUNCHY WHOLEMEAL ROLLS

This recipe will make 16 to 20 rolls which can be eaten as soon as they have cooled or may be frozen for future use.

Imperial (Metric)	American
2 oz (55g) whole or cracked wheat grains	¼ cupful whole or cracked wheat grains
2 tablespoonsful malt extract	2 tablespoonsful malt extract
¼ pint (140ml) water	⅔ cupful hot water
1 oz (30g) fresh yeast	2½ tablespoonsful fresh yeast
1½-1¾ pints (850-1000ml) warm water	3¾-4¼ cupsful warm water
3 lbs (1.35 kilos) wholemeal flour	12 cupsful wholewheat flour
1 tablespoonful sea salt	1 tablespoonful sea salt
2 tablespoonsful vegetable oil .	2 tablespoonsful vegetable oil
¼ pint (140ml) milk	⅔ cupful milk
2 tablespoonsful sesame seeds	2 tablespoonsful sesame seeds

1. Soak the wheat and malt extract in the hot water for several hours or overnight.

2. Stir the yeast into a cupful of the warm water and leave until it begins to froth.

3. Mix the flour and salt in a warmed bowl.

4. Stir into the flour and rest of the water, the yeast mixture, and the soaked wheat and malt extract.

5. Knead on a floured board for 10 minutes until a smooth dough is formed.

6. Return to the mixing bowl, cover with a cloth and leave to rise in a warm place for about 1½ hours or until doubled in size.

7. Knead again on a floured board for a few minutes then divide into equal pieces and form into rolls.

8. Lay out on greased trays and decorate the tops by brushing with milk and sprinkling with sesame seeds.

9. Cover and leave to rise again for 20 minutes in a warm place.

10. Bake in a pre-heated oven at 425°F/220°C (Gas Mark 7) for 20-30 minutes.

11. Turn onto wire racks and cool.

2.

KEBABS

Kebabs, like sausages and burgers, are an essential part of any barbecue. Most vegetables can be cooked in this way and can be supplemented by burger mix formed into balls and skewered alongside them. Try whole mushrooms, chunks of onion, pepper, aubergine (eggplant), tomato, celery and small potatoes. Firmer vegetables such as potatoes and onions can first be softened by blanching in boiling water for a few minutes. Fruits can also be combined with vegetables or burger mixes, in particular pineapple, banana, orange, peaches, figs and mangoes.

Cook kebabs over a medium heat turning frequently. Remember that, with meaty kebabs, the meat supplies the fat for sealing and cooking, but with the vegetarian version you will need to baste occasionally with good quality vegetable oil or butter. To do this, keep a cup of oil or melted butter and a pastry brush handy. Remove the kebab from the grill when basting. Alternatively, you can marinate the vegetables beforehand and baste with some of the marinade during cooking.

Have all the foods you intend to cook prepared beforehand. For a do-it-yourself barbecue you can provide your guests with the skewers and the ingredients in bowls and let them choose and cook their own combinations.

Kebabs can be served as they are or with a sauce or relish — recipes for which will be found later in the book.

BASIC VEGETABLE KEBAB

Imperial (Metric)	American
2 large aubergines	2 large eggplants
½ lb (225g) tiny onions	1½ cupsful tiny onions
2 green peppers	2 green peppers
½ lb (225g) button mushrooms	4 cupsful button mushrooms
6 tomatoes	6 tomatoes
Vegetable oil	Vegetable oil
Sea salt and freshly ground black pepper	Sea salt and freshly ground black pepper

1. Slice the aubergines (eggplants) into 1-inch (2.5cm) cubes, sprinkle with sea salt and place in a colander to drain for 20 minutes.

2. Rinse the aubergine (eggplant) cubes in cold running water.

3. Meanwhile, skin the onions then cook them with the aubergines (eggplants) for 10 minutes in boiling water.

4. Wash and remove the seeds from the peppers and cut into 1-inch (2.5cm) squares.

5. Wipe the mushrooms clean with a kitchen towel or tissue and halve the tomatoes.

6. Skewer all the vegetables and baste with the oil.

7. Sprinkle with sea salt or garlic salt and freshly ground black pepper and cook over a medium-hot fire.

8. Baste with more oil from time to time and after 15 minutes or so they should be ready to serve.

MUSHROOM AND TOMATO KEBABS

Imperial (Metric)	American
½ lb (225g) small tomatoes	8 ounces small tomatoes
½ lb (225g) button mushrooms	4 cupsful button mushrooms
4 oz (115g) tiny onions	1 cupful tiny onions
Basic Marinade (page 42)	Basic Marinade (page 42)

1. Peel the tomatoes and cut into quarters.

2. Clean the mushrooms with a kitchen towel and peel the onions.

3. Marinate all the ingredients for 2 hours.

4. Skewer the ingredients and baste with more of the marinade while cooking.

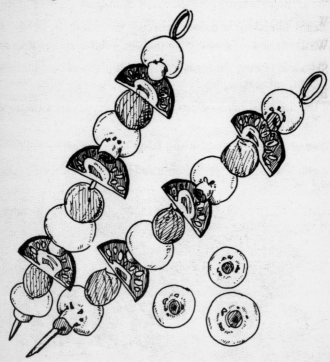

GREEN TOMATO KEBABS

Imperial (Metric)	American
1 clove garlic	1 clove garlic
½ teaspoonful sea salt	½ teaspoonful sea salt
¼ pint (140ml) vegetable oil	⅔ cupful vegetable oil
1 lb (455g) large green tomatoes	1 pound large green tomatoes
4 oz (115g) tiny onions	1 cupful tiny onions
2 red peppers	2 red peppers

1. Skin the garlic and slice thinly with a sharp knife.

2. Sprinkle salt over the garlic and grind to a pulp with the back of a spoon.

3. Mix the garlic pulp into the oil and leave to stand for an hour or so.

4. Wash and slice the green tomatoes thickly.

5. Wash and de-seed the peppers and cut into 1-inch (2.5cm) squares.

6. Skewer and brush with the garlic oil.

7. Baste frequently during cooking with more of the oil.

FRUITY KEBABS

Imperial (Metric)	American
4 oz (115g) tiny onions *or* shallots	1 cupful tiny onions *or* shallots
1 medium green pepper	1 medium green pepper
½ lb (225g) pineapple cubes, fresh or tinned	1¾ cupsful pineapple cubes, fresh or canned
2 peaches *or* 1 × 7 oz (200g) tin peach slices	2 peaches *or* 7 ounces canned peach slices
1 large orange divided into segments	1 large orange divided into segments

1. Blanch the skinned onions or shallots in boiling water for 5 minutes.

2. Wash and remove the seeds from the pepper and cut into ¾-inch (2cm) squares.

3. Cut the pineapple into cubes if not already prepared and slice the peaches.

4. Skewer and baste the prepared ingredients with marinade or vegetable oil and cook.

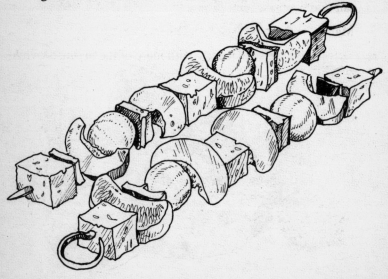

BANANA KEBABS

Although the combination of banana, onion and tomato in this recipe sounds rather unlikely it is in fact quite delicious.

Imperial (Metric)
4 oz (115g) tiny onions
3 firm bananas
½ lb (225g) small tomatoes
¼ pint (140ml) good quality
  vegetable oil
2 tablespoonsful fresh lemon juice
½ tablespoonful white wine vinegar
½ teaspoonful garlic salt
1 tablespoonful chopped basil

American
1 cupful tiny onions
3 firm bananas
8 ounces small tomatoes
⅔ cupful good quality vegetable oil
2 tablespoonsful fresh lemon juice
½ tablespoonful white wine vinegar
½ teaspoonful garlic salt
1 tablespoonful chopped basil

1. Skin and blanch the onions by boiling for 5 minutes.

2. Peel and cut the bananas into ½-inch (1cm) slices.

3. Peel the tomatoes by dipping briefly into boiling water then halve.

4. Prepare a marinade by mixing the oil, lemon juice, vinegar, garlic salt and chopped basil.

5. Marinate all the prepared ingredients for 2 hours.

6. Skewer and baste frequently with more of the marinade while cooking.

BASIC MARINADE FOR VEGETABLES

Imperial (Metric)
½ pint (285ml) good quality
  vegetable oil
¼ pint (140ml) white wine vinegar
  or cider vinegar
Sea salt
Freshly ground black pepper
1 teaspoonful soft raw cane sugar

American
1⅓ cupsful good quality vegetable
  oil
⅔ cupful white wine vinegar *or* cider
  vinegar
Sea salt
Freshly ground black pepper
1 teaspoonful soft raw cane sugar

1. Mix all the ingredients together and leave to stand for an hour or so, stirring occasionally until the sugar is dissolved.

2. Pour over the vegetables or fruit before they are skewered and leave to marinate for 2 hours.

3. Skewer the food and cook over a medium grill.

4. Brush the kebabs with the marinade every few minutes until the food is tender.

MARINADE WITH HERBS AND GARLIC

Imperial (Metric)
2 medium cloves garlic
½ teaspoonful sea salt
1 cupful olive *or* walnut oil
Juice of 2 lemons
Freshly ground black pepper
1 teaspoonful soft raw cane sugar
1 tablespoonful fresh oregano,
  chopped (*or* ½ tablespoonful
  dried)
1 tablespoonful fresh basil, chopped
  (*or* ½ tablespoonful dried)

American
2 medium cloves garlic
½ teaspoonful sea salt
1¼ cupsful olive *or* walnut oil
Juice of 2 lemons
Freshly ground black pepper
1 teaspoonful soft raw cane sugar
1 tablespoonful fresh oregano,
  chopped (*or* ½ tablespoonful
  dried)
1 tablespoonful fresh basil, chopped
  (*or* ½ tablespoonful dried)

1. Slice and crush the garlic with the sea salt.

2. Mix the garlic into the oil then add the lemon juice.

3. Season with pepper and then add the sugar.

4. Allow to stand, but stir every few minutes until the sugar has dissolved.

5. Lastly, stir in the fresh chopped herbs. Leave for at least 1 hour before use so that the flavours have time to mingle.

6. Marinate the vegetables following the instructions in the basic recipe (page 42).

ORANGE MARINADE

Imperial (Metric)	American
1/2 pint (285ml) cold-pressed olive oil	1 1/3 cupsful cold-pressed olive oil
2 1/2 fl oz (75ml) white wine	5 tablespoonsful white wine
1/4 pint (140ml) fresh orange juice	2/3 cupsful fresh orange juice
Sea salt and freshly ground black pepper	Sea salt and freshly ground black pepper
1/2 teaspoonful soft raw cane sugar	1/2 teaspoonful soft raw cane sugar

1. Beat all the ingredients together with a whisk and leave to stand for an hour or so, stirring occasionally until the sugar is dissolved.

2. To use, marinate the kebab ingredients for at least 2 hours.

3. Skewer the food and cook over a medium grill.

4. Brush with the marinade every few minutes until the food is done.

3.

BARBECUED VEGETABLE DISHES

BAKED POTATOES

This is the basic method for baking potatoes on a barbecue. There are many ways of varying this and of making the end result more exciting. Some ideas for these variations follow.

Imperial (Metric)	American
1 medium to large potato per person	1 medium to large potato per person
Vegetable oil	Vegetable oil
Sea salt and freshly ground black pepper	Sea salt and freshly ground black pepper
Butter	Butter

1. Choose firm, medium-sized baking potatoes and scrub.

2. Brush each potato with vegetable oil and wrap in a piece of foil, folding the edges together to seal.

3. Bake for 45-60 minutes with the grill right on top of the charcoal, turning occasionally.

4. When the potatoes are soft, split with a knife and push the ends to fluff.

5. Season with salt and pepper, and serve with a generous amount of butter or polyunsaturated vegetable margarine.

Serving suggestions:
- Lemon and Parsley Butter (page 107).
- Cream cheese and chopped chives.

- Chopped parsley with cottage cheese.
- Remove the insides, mash with hard-boiled egg, butter, herbs and seasonings and return to their skins.

BAKED POTATOES WITH ONIONS

Imperial (Metric)	American
6 medium potatoes	6 medium potatoes
2 medium onions	2 medium onions
4 oz (115g) butter *or* vegetable margarine	½ cupful butter *or* vegetable margarine
Sea salt and freshly ground black pepper	Sea salt and freshly ground black pepper

1. Scrub the potatoes but do not remove their skins.

2. Cut each potato in half lengthwise.

3. Remove the onion skins then cut into slices.

4. Place a few onion slices and a knob of butter between the halves of each potato.

5. Wrap each potato in a square of foil and seal by making a double fold around the edges.

6. Place on the grill close to the hot charcoal and bake for 45 to 60 minutes until tender. Turn once during cooking.

7. Serve with more butter, sea salt and freshly ground black pepper.

CHEESY POTATOES

Try this novel way of baking potatoes. The ingredients are for one portion.

Imperial (Metric)	American
1 potato	1 potato
A few thin slices of onion	A few thin slices of onion
¼ teaspoonful celery salt	¼ teaspoonful celery salt
Freshly ground black pepper	Freshly ground black pepper
2 tablespoonsful Cheddar cheese	2 tablespoonsful Cheddar cheese
1 tablespoonful butter *or*	1 tablespoonful butter *or*
polyunsaturated margarine	polyunsaturated margarine

1. Peel the potatoes.

2. Cut each potato lengthwise into ¼-inch (6mm) slices and then again across as if you were making chips.

3. Prepare a double thickness of foil for each potato and pile the potato chips onto the foil.

4. Sprinkle each potato liberally with a little onion, celery salt, freshly ground pepper, and grated Cheddar cheese. Make sure all the surfaces are seasoned.

5. Dot with 1 tablespoonful butter or margarine.

6. Seal by folding the edges of the foil together, but allow plenty of room for expansion of steam.

7. Cook on the grill for about 30 minutes or until tender, turning occasionally.

8. Serve in their foil wrapping.

SKILLET POTATOES
Serves 6.

Imperial (Metric)	American
2½ fl oz (75ml) vegetable oil	¼ cupful vegetable oil
6 medium potatoes, cooked and diced	6 medium potatoes, cooked and diced
2 cupsful sliced onions	2½ cupsful sliced onions
2 tablespoonsful chopped parsley	2 tablespoonsful chopped parsley
2 tablespoonsful chopped pimento	2 tablespoonsful chopped pimento
½ teaspoonful sea salt	½ teaspoonful sea salt
Freshly ground black pepper	Freshly ground black pepper

1. Heat the oil in a skillet (heavy bottomed frying pan) over gentle heat.

2. Combine the potatoes, sliced onions, parsley and pimento in the skillet.

3. Add seasoning to taste.

4. Cook slowly, turning occasionally until golden brown and crisp.

CORN ON THE COB

Imperial (Metric)	American
1 cob of fresh corn per person	1 cob of fresh corn per person
Butter or vegetable margarine	Butter or vegetable margarine
Sea salt and freshly ground black pepper	Sea salt and freshly ground black pepper

1. Remove the husks and silk from fresh corn cobs.

2. Place each cob on a piece of aluminium foil and spread with plenty of soft butter or margarine.

3. Sprinkle with sea salt and freshly ground pepper.

4. Wrap the foil tightly around each cob, but do not seal completely, because the corn should be roasted rather than steamed.

5. Place on the grill over hot charcoal and cook for 15 to 20 minutes or until the corn is succulent and tender.

6. Turn the cobs frequently to avoid burning.

7. Serve with more butter, sea salt, and freshly ground pepper.

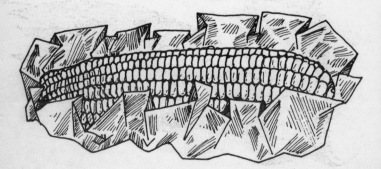

SWEETCORN INDIAN-STYLE

For this recipe you will need freshly picked sweetcorn with the green outer husks still in place.

Imperial (Metric)
1 fresh corn cob per person
Butter, freshly ground black pepper
   and sea salt to taste

American
1 fresh corn cob per person
Butter, freshly ground black pepper
   and sea salt to taste

1. Pull back the green husks and pull away the strands of silk.

2. Fold the husks back in position.

3. Place on the grill over hot charcoal and roast, turning frequently, for 15 to 20 minutes or till husks are dry and the corn inside is beginning to brown.

4. Serve with butter, pepper and salt.

SWEETCORN OFF THE COB

Imperial (Metric)	American
½ lb (225g) fresh corn stripped from the cob *or* ½ lb (225g) frozen sweetcorn	1½ cupsful fresh corn stripped from the cob *or* 1½ cupsful frozen sweetcorn kernels
2 oz (55g) butter	¼ cupful butter
Sea salt and freshly ground black pepper	Sea salt and freshly ground black pepper

1. Make an 18-inch (45cm) square of double thickness aluminium foil.

2. Shape it around your fist to make a container and fill this with the sweetcorn.

3. Season with sea salt and freshly ground pepper and top with the butter.

4. Fold up the edges of the foil and seal, leaving a space for the steam to expand.

5. Place on the grill and cook for 15 to 20 minutes, turning occasionally.

SWEETCORN CHEESE FRY
Serves 4-6.

Sweetcorn with a creamy sauce of butter and herbs grilled over charcoal and topped with cheese! Use any good quality Cheddar cheese or Gruyère.

Imperial (Metric)
2 tablespoonsful butter *or* polyunsaturated margarine
3 cupsful fresh or frozen sweetcorn
¼ pint (140ml) single cream
2 tablespoonsful chopped chives
1 clove garlic
½ teaspoonful sea salt
Freshly ground black pepper
2 oz (55g) Cheddar cheese, grated

American
2 tablespoonsful butter *or* polyunsaturated margarine
3¾ cupsful fresh or frozen sweetcorn
⅔ cupful light cream
2 tablespoonsful chopped chives
1 clove garlic
½ teaspoonful sea salt
Freshly ground black pepper
½ cupful grated Cheddar cheese

1. Prepare a container by taking a length of about 3 feet (91cm) of aluminium foil 18 inches (45cm) wide and fold in half to make a square then fold up the edges to make a pouch.

2. In the centre place the butter or margarine, corn, cream, chives, and crushed garlic.

3. Add the salt and season with freshly ground pepper to taste. Stir the ingredients together.

4. Fold in the edges of the foil and seal tightly.

5. Place on the grill over a gentle heat and cook for about 10 to 15 minutes.

6. Remove from the heat and open foil. Sprinkle with grated cheese and, once this has melted, serve straight away.

CREAMY CORN

Imperial (Metric)	American
3 oz (85g) cream cheese	1/3 cupful cream cheese
2 1/2 fl oz (75ml) milk	1/4 cupful milk
1 tablespoonful butter *or* polyunsaturated margarine	1 tablespoonful butter *or* polyunsaturated margarine
1/2 teaspoonful onion salt	1/2 teaspoonful onion salt
2 cupful sweetcorn	2 1/2 cupful sweetcorn

1. Combine the cream cheese, milk, butter or margarine, and onion salt in a skillet.

2. Stir mixture over low coals till the cheese melts.

3. Add the corn; heat through and serve, garnishing with parsley or a sprinkle of paprika.

BARBECUE PEAS WITH MUSHROOMS

Imperial (Metric)
1 lb (455g) fresh or frozen peas
Sea salt and freshly ground black
   pepper
3 tablespoonsful butter *or*
   polyunsaturated margarine
4 oz (115g) fresh mushrooms

American
1 pound fresh or frozen peas
Sea salt and freshly ground black
   pepper
3 tablespoonsful butter *or*
   polyunsaturated margarine
2 cupsful fresh mushrooms

1. Using double thickness aluminium foil make a 12-inch (30cm) square then shape with the fist to make a container.

2. Place the peas in this and season with salt and pepper.

3. Add the mushrooms and the butter or margarine.

4. Fold up the edges of the foil leaving a space for the steam to expand, and seal by folding tightly.

5. Place over hot charcoal and cook for 10 to 15 minutes turning occasionally.

BARBECUED BROCCOLI

This works equally well for green broccoli spears or ordinary cauliflower although this should be split into separate florets.

Imperial (Metric)	American
1 lb (455g) fresh broccoli	1 pound fresh broccoli
Sea salt	Sea salt
Freshly ground black pepper	Freshly ground black pepper
1 lemon	1 lemon
2 oz (55g) butter *or* polyunsaturated margarine	¼ cupful butter *or* polyunsaturated margarine

1. Place the broccoli spears on a large square of double-thickness aluminium foil.

2. Season with salt and pepper and add thin slices of lemon or sprinkle with 1 tablespoonful lemon juice.

3. Chop the butter into small pieces and dot all over the broccoli.

4. Seal the edges of the foil by doubling them over, but leave a little space for expansion of the steam.

5. Heat over the barbecue for about 20 minutes, turning frequently.

6. Serve when just tender.

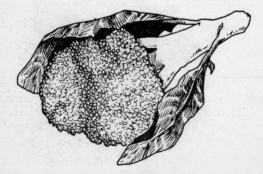

CHEESE AND TOMATO BAKE

Imperial (Metric)	American
4 large tomatoes	4 large tomatoes
Sea salt and freshly ground black pepper	Sea salt and freshly ground black pepper
¼ cupful soft wholemeal breadcrumbs	¼ cupful soft wholewheat breadcrumbs
¼ cupful grated Cheddar cheese	¼ cupful grated Cheddar cheese
1 tablespoonful butter *or* polyunsaturated margarine, melted	1 tablespoonful butter *or* polyunsaturated margarine, melted
1 tablespoonful chopped parsley	1 tablespoonful chopped parsley

1. Cut the tomatoes in half with a zig-zag cut, as for a salad.

2. Season well with sea salt and freshly ground pepper.

3. In a bowl mix the breadcrumbs, cheese, butter, and parsley and sprinkle over the tomato halves.

4. Heat the tomatoes on foil over hot charcoal until they begin to soften.

5. Garnish with a sprig of parsley and serve immediately.

BAKED TOMATOES

Imperial (Metric)	American
4 medium tomatoes	4 medium tomatoes
Sea salt	Sea salt
Tabasco sauce	*Tabasco* sauce
Freshly ground black pepper	Freshly ground black pepper
1 medium onion	1 medium onion

1. Select firm tomatoes and cut each in half crosswise, sprinkling with sea salt, *Tabasco* sauce and freshly ground pepper.

2. Place the cut halves together again, with a thin slice of onion in between.

3. Wrap each tomato in a square of heavy aluminium foil.

4. Heat at the edge of the grill for 15 to 20 minutes.

TOMATOES WITH HERBS
Serves 6.

Imperial (Metric)	American
6 ripe tomatoes	6 ripe tomatoes
1 teaspoonful sea salt	1 teaspoonful sea salt
¼ teaspoonful coarse black pepper	¼ teaspoonful coarse black pepper
1 teaspoonful chopped fresh thyme	1 teaspoonful chopped fresh thyme
¼ cupful chopped fresh parsley	¼ cupful chopped fresh parsley
¼ cupful chopped fresh chives	¼ cupful chopped fresh chives
⅓ pint (200ml) salad oil	¾ cupful salad oil
2½ fl oz (75ml) tarragon vinegar	¼ cupful tarragon vinegar

1. Peel the tomatoes by dipping briefly in boiling water. The skins should come away easily.

2. Place the tomatoes in a bowl and sprinkle with seasonings and herbs.

3. Combine the oil and vinegar and pour over.

4. Cover and allow to stand for at least 1 hour, spooning the dressing over the tomatoes from time to time.

5. Wrap in aluminium foil and heat for 10 to 15 minutes over a medium barbecue.

GRILL-TOP TOMATOES

Imperial (Metric)	American
4 large tomatoes	4 large tomatoes
Basic Marinade (page 42)	Basic Marinade (page 42)
Sea salt	Sea salt
Freshly ground black pepper	Freshly ground black pepper
2 tablespoonsful chopped fresh basil	2 tablespoonsful chopped fresh basil

1. Cut the tomatoes in half.

2. Brush the cut surfaces with the marinade and sprinkle with salt, ground pepper, and basil.

3. Place cut side up on aluminium foil over the grill for about 10 minutes or until they begin to soften, but do not turn.

BARBECUE TOMATO AND AUBERGINE SLICES
Serves 6.

Imperial (Metric)	American
3 medium aubergines	3 medium eggplants
Sea salt	Sea salt
2 oz (55g) butter *or* polyunsaturated margarine	¼ cupful butter *or* polyunsaturated margarine
6 oz (170g) Cheddar or Gruyère cheese, grated	1¾ cupsful grated Cheddar or Gruyère cheese
2 large tomatoes	2 large tomatoes
Freshly ground black pepper	Freshly ground black pepper

1. Cut the aubergines (eggplants) into ½-inch (2cm) thick slices and sprinkle with sea salt, then leave in a colander to drain for 1 hour.

2. Wash the aubergine (eggplant) slices and pat dry.

3. Warm the butter in a skillet or frying pan and fry the aubergine (eggplant) slices until tender.

4. Arrange half of the slices on a large sheet of aluminium foil.

5. Top each piece of aubergine (eggplant) with a thin slice of cheese, then a slice of tomato.

6. Sprinkle with sea salt and freshly ground pepper then add more cheese and finally cover with another slice of aubergine (eggplant).

7. Wrap carefully in the foil and seal.

8. Place over a moderately hot barbecue and cook for 20 minutes.

9. Unwrap carefully and serve.

BAKED ONIONS

Imperial (Metric)	American
6 small to medium onions *or* shallots	6 small to medium onions *or* shallots
1 oz (30g) butter	2½ tablespoonful butter
Sea salt	Sea salt

1. Peel the onions and place on a piece of foil large enough to contain them.

2. Cut up the butter and sprinkle pieces over onions.

3. Season with sea salt.

4. Seal securely in the foil and cook over a medium grill until soft, which should take 20 to 30 minutes.

Note: To cook onions for serving with hamburgers, cut into slices and follow the same instructions.

BAKED COURGETTES

Imperial (Metric)	American
2 cupsful sliced courgettes	2½ cupsful sliced zucchini
1 small onion, sliced	1 small onion, sliced
½ clove garlic, sliced	½ clove garlic, sliced
1 oz (30g) butter *or* polyunsaturated margarine	2½ tablespoonsful butter *or* polyunsaturated margarine
½ teaspoonful sea salt	½ teaspoonful sea salt
Freshly ground black pepper	Freshly ground black pepper
2 tablespoonsful grated Cheddar cheese	2 tablespoonsful grated Cheddar cheese

1. Wrap all the ingredients except the cheese securely in a double thickness of foil.

2. Cook over a cool part of the fire for 15 to 25 minutes, by which time the courgettes (zucchini) should be soft.

3. Sprinkle with cheese, stir and serve.

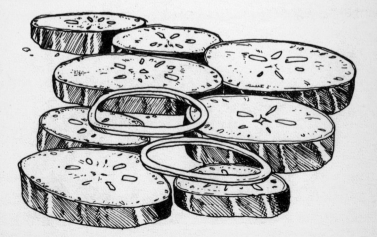

AVOCADO MUSHROOMS

Imperial (Metric)	American
½ lb (225g) mushrooms	4 cupsful mushrooms
1 avocado	1 avocado
Freshly ground black pepper	Freshly ground black pepper
Sea salt	Sea salt
Freshly squeezed lemon juice	Freshly squeezed lemon juice
1 clove garlic	1 clove garlic
2 oz (55g) Cheddar cheese, grated	½ cupful grated Cheddar cheese
Butter	Butter

1. Prepare the mushrooms by gently wiping with a dry kitchen towel and removing the stems.

2. Prepare the filling by mashing the avocado flesh with the rest of the ingredients except the cheese.

3. Place the filling in the mushrooms and top with a knob of butter and a little grated cheese.

4. Wrap individual portions of three or four mushrooms in a double thickness of foil.

5. Bake over a moderate heat for 15 to 20 minutes, sprinkle with cheese and serve.

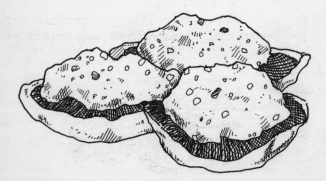

BASIC NUT STUFFING FOR VEGETABLES

Several of the following recipes use this basic mixture which can, of course, be varied as you wish. You could add grated cheese, cooked brown rice, cooked left-over vegetables etc.

Imperial (Metric)	American
2 medium onions	2 medium onions
2 tablespoonsful vegetable oil	2 tablespoonsful vegetable oil
½ lb (225g) nuts	1¼ cupsful nuts
1 cupful wholemeal breadcrumbs	1¼ cupful wholewheat breadcrumbs
1 tablespoonful chopped parsley	1 tablespoonful chopped parsley
1 teaspoonful chopped thyme	1 teaspoonful chopped thyme
Sea salt and freshly ground black pepper	Sea salt and freshly ground black pepper
1 oz (30g) vegetable margarine	2½ tablespoonsful vegetable margarine
2 eggs	2 eggs
1 tablespoonful tomato purée	1 tablespoonful tomato paste

1. Chop the onions and fry in a little vegetable oil, but do not allow to brown.

2. Put the nuts through a mincer or briefly liquidize. The idea is to chop them into small pieces without reducing them to paste.

3. Add the nuts to the breadcrumbs in a mixing bowl and stir in the chopped herbs, salt and pepper. Now add the cooked onion and rub in the margarine.

4. Mix in the two eggs which should bind the ingredients and give a workable consistency. Add the tomato purée and a little water if necessary.

STUFFED MARROW

Imperial (Metric)	American
Basic Stuffing (page 63)	Basic Stuffing (page 63)
1 medium marrow	1 medium summer squash
2 large tomatoes	2 large tomatoes
2 fl oz (60ml) vegetable oil *or* melted butter	¼ cupful vegetable oil *or* melted butter

1. Prepare the basic stuffing.

2. Remove the ends of the marrow (squash) and cut into 2½-inch (6cm) wide slices.

3. Scoop out the seeds with a spoon.

4. Stuff each slice with the stuffing and top with a thick slice of tomato.

5. Brush with oil or melted butter and wrap in a double thickness of foil as individual portions.

6. Cook over a medium heat for 20 to 30 minutes.

STUFFED PEPPERS

Imperial (Metric)
Basic Stuffing (page 63)
4 large green peppers
2 fl oz (60ml) vegetable oil *or*
melted butter

American
Basic Stuffing (page 63)
4 large green peppers
¼ cupful vegetable oil *or* melted
butter

1. Prepare the basic nut stuffing.

2. Select large, perfect peppers. Wash and slice off the tops and remove all the seeds.

3. Stuff the peppers and replace the tops.

4. Brush with melted butter or oil and wrap in a double thickness of foil.

5. Cook slowly for 30 minutes.

Note: Cabbage leaves, tomatoes, globe artichokes, and large mushrooms can all be stuffed in the same way.

MUSHROOMS BAKED WITH HERBS

Imperial (Metric)	American
½ lb (225g) button mushrooms	4 cupsful button mushrooms
2 tablespoonsful finely chopped onion	2 tablespoonsful finely chopped onion
2 tablespoonsful butter *or* polyunsaturated vegetable margarine	2 tablespoonsful butter *or* polyunsaturated vegetable margarine
½ cupful chopped parsley	½ cupful chopped parsley
1 tablespoonful chopped thyme	1 tablespoonful chopped thyme
2 tablespoonsful fresh lemon juice	2 tablespoonsful fresh lemon juice
Sea salt	Sea salt
Freshly ground black pepper	Freshly ground black pepper

1. Wrap all the ingredients in a double thickness of foil.

2. Cook gently over a medium barbecue for 20 to 30 minutes, by which time the mushrooms should be soft and the flavours combined.

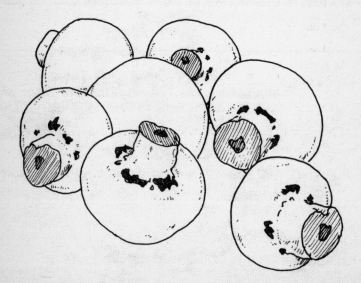

STUFFED CABBAGE LEAVES

Imperial (Metric)	**American**
1 small savoy cabbage	1 small savoy cabbage
2 medium onions	2 medium onions
2 oz (55g) mushrooms	1 cupful mushrooms
2 tablesponsful vegetable oil	2 tablesponsful vegetable oil
1 cupful cooked brown rice	1¼ cupful cooked brown rice
2 tablespoonsful chopped nuts	2 tablespoonsful chopped nuts
Sea salt and freshly ground black pepper	Sea salt and freshly ground black pepper
2 tablespoonsful grated cheese	2 tablespoonsful grated cheese
2 tomatoes	2 tomatoes
½ pint (285ml) vegetable stock	1⅓ cupful vegetable stock

1. To prepare the cabbage cut off the stem and peel off the leaves intact, then place them in boiling water for a few minutes to soften.

2. Chop one of the onions and all the mushrooms and fry in the oil.

3. After a few minutes stir in the rice, chopped nuts and seasonings.

4. Remove from the heat and spoon in the grated cheese mixing well.

5. Lay out the cabbage leaves and divide the stuffing.

6. Roll each leaf around the stuffing and place on an individual piece of foil.

7. Slice the remaining onion and fry for a few minutes. When soft lay over the cabbage rolls together with slices of tomato.

8. Pour 2 tablespoonsful of stock over each roll and seal the edges of the foil.

9. Cook slowly for at least 30 minutes and serve with apple sauce or sweet pickles.

BAKED RICE WITH MUSHROOMS

Imperial (Metric)	American
2 cupsful cooked brown rice	2½ cupsful cooked brown rice
4 oz (115g) button mushrooms	2 cupsful button mushrooms
1 cupful cold water	1 cupful cold water
1 medium onion, chopped	1 medium onion, chopped
1 teaspoonful soya sauce	1 teaspoonful soy sauce
Few drops *Tabasco* sauce	Few drops *Tabasco* sauce
½ teaspoonful butter *or*	½ teaspoonful butter *or*
polyunsaturated margarine	polyunsaturated margarine

1. Take a 3 foot (90cm) length of foil and fold it in half.

2. Form the foil into a container around your fist.

3. Add the rice, mushrooms, water, onion, and seasonings.

4. Stir to mix the ingredients and top with butter.

5. Fold the edges of the foil to seal tightly.

6. Place on a grill over hot coals and heat for 15 to 20 minutes.

7. Before serving, open the foil and add an extra pat of butter and fluff up the rice with fork.

CHILLI BEANS

This is a vegetarian version of Chilli con Carne which you can prepare in the kitchen beforehand and then heat up on the barbecue.

Imperial (Metric)	American
¾ lb (340g) red kidney beans	2 cupsful red kidney beans
2 onions	2 onions
2 tablespoonsful butter	2 tablespoonsful butter
2-3 large aubergines	2-3 large eggplants
2½ fl oz (75ml) vegetable oil	¼ cupful vegetable oil
1 lb (455g) tomatoes	1 pound tomatoes
Sea salt and freshly ground black pepper	Sea salt and freshly ground black pepper
2 cloves garlic, crushed	2 cloves garlic, crushed
1 teaspoonful ground coriander	1 teaspoonful ground coriander
Chilli powder	Chilli powder

1. Soak the beans overnight and cook for 1½ hours, or ½ hour in a pressure cooker. (Alternatively, use 2 tins of red kidney beans).

2. Fry the onions in the butter in a heavy iron pan and when soft add the diced aubergine (eggplant) and some of the oil.

3. The aubergines (eggplants) will soak up the oil, so keep adding more as they do so.

4. When the aubergines (eggplants) are soft add the tomatoes, salt, pepper, garlic and spices.

5. Add the chilli powder, starting with a very small amount, just enough to cover the tip of a knife.

6. After 15 minutes cooking add the cooked beans and simmer for a further ½ hour over a very gentle heat.

7. Add more chilli powder to taste but be careful, there is nothing you can do if too much is added. Serve with sausages or hamburgers.

BARBECUE BAKED BEANS

A vegetarian version of this simple and popular dish which is so useful for serving with hamburgers and other barbecue food. This is another recipe which you can prepare well beforehand then reheat on the barbecue before serving.

Imperial (Metric)	American
2 oz (55g) *Sosmix*	1 cupful *Sosmix*
1 oz (30g) butter *or* polyunsaturated margarine	2½ tablespoonsful butter *or* polyunsaturated margarine
½ cupful onion, finely chopped	½ cupful onion, finely chopped
½ cupful mushrooms, finely chopped	½ cupful mushrooms, finely chopped
1 lb (455g) baked beans	2 cupsful baked beans
1 tablespoonful horse-radish sauce	1 tablespoonful horse-radish sauce
1 teaspoonful French mustard	1 teaspoonful French mustard

1. Mix the *Sosmix* with enough cold water to make a sticky dough.

2. Melt the butter in a frying pan and sauté the chopped onion and mushrooms until soft.

3. Add the *Sosmix* and stir so that it breaks up and mixes with the mushroom and onion.

4. Cook for five minutes stirring frequently then add the remaining ingredients.

5. Heat gently and stir to mix all the ingredients.

6. Re-heat on the barbecue and serve.

4.

WOK COOKERY

The wok is a hemispherical frying pan made of plate steel. It comes with a lid and often a stand or collar for adapting it to use on an ordinary gas cooker. It is most often employed for the Chinese method of cooking known as stir-frying, but is much used in Chinese cookery in general as a utility pan for braising, steaming, shallow-frying and deep-frying. A wok is particularly useful for barbecue cooking on charcoal or on an open fire, where, because of its sturdy nature, it is unaffected by extremes of heat or rough treatment. Whereas you would *not* want to use your best stainless steel pan for cooking over an open fire the wok is ideally suited to this type of cooking.

Caring for Your Wok
The traditional wok is made of mild steel and is prone to rusting, although in the Chinese kitchen it is in such frequent use that it hardly has the chance to do so. As soon as you buy a wok it should be washed in hot soapy water to remove any grease or lacquer with which it may have been protected. Dry carefully and stand in a warm place for half an hour then rub inside and out with vegetable oil. This should be repeated after each use. The best method of cleaning is to fill it with water when hot and remove any stubborn pieces of food with a bamboo brush. It is not a good idea to use harsh scourers on a wok as, with a little use, it will develop a dark coating which helps protect it and prevents the food sticking.

Barbecue Cooking with a Wok
When barbecue cooking with a wok the stand is useful in steadying it and in keeping it from direct contact with the hot coals. For stir-

frying the ingredients are finely chopped and put in the pan with some heated oil or butter; two or three tablespoonsful are quite sufficient for a panful of vegetables or rice. The cooking need only be very brief but should be accompanied by frequent stirring with a wooden spatula so that all the surfaces of the food are exposed to the hot metal of the pan. The rounded shape of the wok is well suited to stir-frying, as food displaced from the centre is replaced by food tumbling in from the sloping sides. The idea is to expose the food to a short sharp burst of heat, so the metal of a wok is intentionally thin allowing it to heat quickly, then cool quickly afterwards so that no deterioration of the food occurs subsequently.

Stir-frying, apart from being a quick and easy method of cooking, is also healthy as, although the heat is fierce, the brief exposure ensures that very little nutritive value is lost and the juices are sealed in. The food also retains more of it's individual taste and texture rather than becoming uniformly bland and mushy which is a characteristic of so much badly cooked Western food.

BASIC BROWN RICE
Several of the following recipes require pre-cooked rice so use this basic method to prepare the rice well before the time you will need it. If properly cooked, the rice grains should remain intact and separate and have a succulent bite to them. Cooked brown rice keeps 3 to 4 days in a cool place, 5 to 7 days in a fridge.

Imperial (Metric)	American
2 cupsful water	2½ cupsful water
1 cupful rice	1¼ cupful rice
½ teaspoonful sea salt	½ teaspoonful sea salt

1. Wash the rice under cold running water.

2. Use a heavy pan with a tightly fitting lid. Put the cold water in the pan with the rice and bring to the boil. Do not add salt at this stage.

3. Reduce the heat and simmer gently keeping the lid in place until cooked. Do not stir.

4. After 45 minutes the water should have evaporated and the rice will just be starting to catch on the bottom.

5. Remove from the heat. Stand for a while and sprinkle with sea salt before using.

BASIC FRIED RICE WITH EGG
Serves 5-6.

This is quick and sustaining and is an ideal basis for a barbecue or camping meal. To make it more special, try some of the additions which follow the main recipe.

Imperial (Metric)	American
3 tablespoonsful vegetable oil	3 tablespoonsful vegetable oil
1 onion, finely chopped	1 onion, finely chopped
2 cupsful pre-cooked brown rice (page 72)	2½ cupsful pre-cooked brown rice (page 72)
2 eggs	2 eggs
Sea salt and freshly ground black pepper	Sea salt and freshly ground black pepper
Soya sauce	Soy sauce
2 tomatoes	2 tomatoes

1. Pre-heat the oil in the wok.

2. Cook the onion, stirring continuously until tender but not brown.

3. Add the rice and fry for a few moments.

4. Break in the eggs and stir so that they are well mixed with the rice.

5. Season with sea salt and pepper and sprinkle with soya sauce if liked.

6. Garnish with thin slices of tomato and serve. Delicious if served with sweet pickle, either stirred in or separate.

FRIED RICE WITH HERBS

To the basic fried rice recipe, add:

Imperial (Metric)	American
2 tablespoonsful chopped parsley	2 tablespoonsful chopped parsley
1 tablespoonful chopped oregano	1 tablespoonful chopped oregano
½ tablespoonful chopped thyme	½ tablespoonful chopped thyme
1 teaspoonful paprika	1 teaspoonful paprika

1. Follow the basic recipe but before serving stir in the herbs and paprika.

FRIED RICE WITH MUSHROOMS

In addition to the basic ingredients you will need:

Imperial (Metric)	American
2 cloves garlic	2 cloves garlic
½ lb (225g) mushrooms	4 cupsful mushrooms
Juice of 1 lemon	Juice of 1 lemon
Sprig parsley	Sprig parsley

1. Chop the garlic and fry with the onion, as in basic recipe.

2. Follow the basic recipe, but when the onion is nearly cooked add the sliced mushroom and sprinkle with lemon juice. Cook for 2 to 3 minutes then proceed as above.

3. Chop the parsley and stir into the rice before serving.

FRIED RICE WITH BEANS
To the basic recipe, add:

Imperial (Metric)
1 cupful cooked red kidney beans *or* aduki beans

American
1¼ cupsful cooked red kidney beans *or* aduki beans

1. Add the beans at the same time as the rice.

FRIED RICE AND VEGETABLES
In addition to the basic ingredients you will need:

Imperial (Metric)
1 carrot
2 sticks celery
1 green pepper
1 tablespoonful chopped parsley
½ tablespoonful chopped marjoram

American
1 carrot
2 celery stalks
1 green pepper
1 tablespoonful chopped parsley
½ tablespoonful chopped marjoram

1. Finely chop the carrot, celery, and pepper and fry in the oil with the onions.

2. Follow the rest of the instructions for the basic recipe and serve as directed.

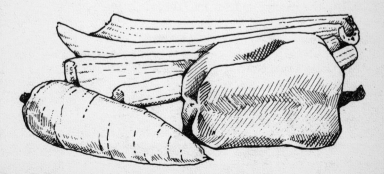

CHINESE STIR-FRIED GREENS

This recipe can be used for all types of leafy greens, including spinach, turnip tops and kale.

Imperial (Metric)	American
1 lb (455g) spring greens *or* cabbage	1 pound spring greens *or* cabbage
2 cloves garlic	2 cloves garlic
3 tablespoonsful vegetable oil	3 tablespoonsful vegetable oil
1 tablespoonful soya sauce	1 tablespoonful soy sauce
2 tablespoonsful vegetable stock	2 tablespoonsful vegetable stock
1 tablespoonful butter	1 tablespoonful butter

1. Wash the greens and remove any tough or dying leaves.

2. Coarsely chop or tear the leaves.

3. Chop the garlic and crush with a little salt between two spoons.

4. Heat the oil in the wok.

5. Add the greens and garlic and stir-fry for 2 minutes.

6. Remove the wok to a cooler part of the fire and add the soya sauce and stock, and cook for 2 minutes.

7. Add the butter, turn several times to distribute, then serve.

STIR-FRIED CABBAGE AND BEANS

To the previous recipe add:

Imperial (Metric)	American
1½ cupsful cooked red kidney beans *or* black-eyed beans	1¾ cupsful cooked red kidney beans *or* black-eyed beans

1. Follow the above but add the beans with the greens and garlic in step 5.

STIR-FRIED MUSHROOMS

Imperial (Metric)	American
1 small cauliflower	1 small cauliflower
1 courgette	1 zucchini
6 spring onions	6 scallions
2 carrots	2 carrots
4 sticks celery	4 celery stalks
4 oz (115g) mushrooms	2 cupsful mushrooms
2 tablespoonsful butter	2 tablespoonsful butter
3 tablespoonsful vegetable stock	3 tablespoonsful vegetable stock
Soya sauce	Soy sauce
Roasted sesame seeds	Roasted sesame seeds

1. Chop the cauliflower into small pieces and slice the courgettes (zucchini), spring onions (scallions), carrots, celery and mushrooms.

2. Melt butter in the wok.

3. Add the vegetables and stir-fry for 5 minutes.

4. Pour in the vegetable stock, place the cover over the wok and cook for 2 minutes.

5. Stir in the soya sauce to taste and serve sprinkled with sesame seeds.

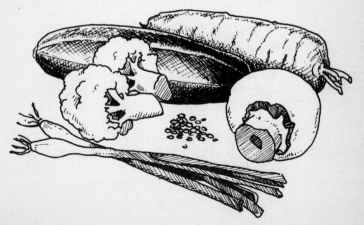

HOT TOSSED SALAD WITH RICE

Imperial (Metric)	American
1 tablespoonful vegetable oil	1 tablespoonful vegetable oil
1 medium lettuce	1 medium lettuce
1 bunch watercress	1 bunch watercress
1 red pepper	1 red pepper
2 cupsful cooked brown rice (page 72)	2½ cupsful cooked brown rice (page 72)
Sea salt and freshly ground black pepper	Sea salt and freshly ground black pepper
2 teaspoonsful lemon juice	2 teaspoonsful lemon juice
Soya sauce	Soy sauce

1. Heat the wok over the barbecue with 1 tablespoonful of vegetable oil.

2. Shred the lettuce and watercress, and slice the tomato.

3. De-seed the red pepper and chop into small squares.

4. Tip the prepared ingredients into the wok and cook for 2 minutes, stirring continuously.

5. Add the rice, seasoning and lemon juice, and cook for a further 2 minutes.

6. Serve with a sprinkling of soya sauce.

5.

OMELETTES AND PANCAKES

A barbecue is an ideal occasion for serving omelettes and pancakes as they need to be done individually and eaten as soon as they are ready.

The main requirement for a successful omelette is for a very hot pan, in fact the oil or butter should be smoking. This will ensure that your omelette rises. When it is done, garnish with thin slices of tomato, cress, lettuce, herbs etc. and be prepared to serve immediately.

Pancakes are ideal for cooking out of doors as, although they are labour intensive and have to be cooked individually, the cook need not be banished to the kitchen to slave over a hot stove, but is free to join in festivities while preparing them. With a little practice you will find pancakes very quick and easy, and very much appreciated by your guests. The key to success is of course the batter, which should be made in advance.

BASIC OMELETTE
Serves 1.

Imperial (Metric)	American
2 eggs	2 eggs
Sea salt	Sea salt
Freshly ground black pepper	Freshly ground black pepper
1 teaspoonful butter *or* vegetable oil	1 teaspoonful butter *or* vegetable oil

1. Use fresh eggs and beat them well with a fork, adding the seasoning and any desired herbs.

2. Set the pan heating with 1 teaspoonful of oil or, preferably, butter.

3. When the butter or oil is beginning to smoke pour in the beaten eggs.

4. Keep lifting the edge of the omelette with a fork to allow more liquid from the top to run underneath and set.

5. Add any filling and continue to cook until the underside begins to brown.

6. When the cooking is finished loosen the edges if stuck, fold in half and serve onto a plate.

HERB OMELETTE

Add 1 tablespoonful of finely chopped fresh herbs such as basil, parsley, thyme, chives, marjoram. A little chopped onion or shallot can also be added.

CHEESE OMELETTE

Gruyère is the best cheese for this purpose although a strongly flavoured Cheddar is quite suitable. Grate 2 oz (55g/½ cupful) into the centre of the omelette before folding. Use plenty of seasoning.

MUSHROOM OMELETTE

Fry ½ thinly sliced onion and 4 or 5 mushrooms, also sliced. Fill the omelette and garnish with a raw sliced mushroom and a sprig of parsley.

MUSHROOM AND CREAM CHEESE OMELETTE

Chop and fry a few large mushrooms. Spread a layer of cream cheese over the partially cooked omelette. Add the mushrooms with extra seasoning then fold and cook for 1 minute more.

TOMATO OMELETTE

Fill the omelette with a layer of very thinly sliced tomatoes sprinkled with sea salt and freshly ground pepper and a good tablespoonful of freshly chopped basil. Top with more sliced tomato and a basil leaf.

RICE OMELETTE
Serves 2.

Imperial (Metric)	American
1 onion, chopped	1 onion, chopped
1 tablespoonful vegetable oil	1 tablespoonful vegetable oil
2 oz (55g) mushrooms	1 cupful mushrooms
1 cupful brown rice, cooked	1¼ cupful brown rice, cooked
3 eggs	3 eggs
Sea salt and freshly ground black pepper	Sea salt and freshly ground black pepper
Soya sauce	Soy sauce

1. First prepare the filling by frying the chopped onion in a little oil until soft.

2. Add the mushrooms and rice and fry for a few more minutes until thoroughly heated, then put aside.

3. Beat the eggs and re-heat the pan with the butter.

4. When the pan is really hot pour in the beaten eggs and, as the bottom layer sets, keep lifting to allow the liquid to flow beneath.

5. When the egg is nearly set sprinkle with ground pepper and sea salt and add the filling with a dash of soya sauce.

6. Fold the omelette and serve.

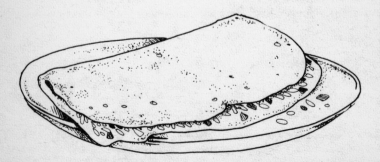

PANCAKE BATTER

The aim is to produce a batter that has a thin, creamy consistency which pours rapidly from a spoon. This will ensure a light delicate pancake.

Imperial (Metric)	American
4 oz (115g) plain 81 per cent wholemeal flour	1 cupful plain 81 per cent wholewheat flour
¼ teaspoonful salt	¼ teaspoonful salt
1 egg	1 egg
½ pint (285ml) milk	1⅓ cupsful milk

1. Sieve the flour and salt into a mixing bowl.

2. Make a well in the centre of the flour and into this crack the egg.

3. Little by little add half of the milk, stirring all the time from the centre with a wooden spoon and gradually incorporate more and more flour from the edges.

4. When a uniform mixture is achieved beat with a whisk to remove any lumps.

5. Whisk in the remainder of the milk and continue to beat for a few minutes to aerate the mixture.

6. Leave to stand in a cool place for at least 20 minutes while the flour absorbs some of the liquid, as this will ensure a smooth, light batter. Cook as described overleaf.

COOKING THE PANCAKE

1. To cook, use a non-stick pan or, preferably, a heavy iron pan which has developed a good black surface from constant oiling before use and no scouring after use.

2. Whisk the batter once more before cooking and pour into a jug.

3. Brush the pan with a little vegetable oil and heat over hot coals until the fat starts to smoke. Pour off any surplus fat.

4. Pour in just enough batter to cover the bottom of the pan, tilting the pan to form an even layer.

5. Cook until the batter begins to bubble then turn with a palette knife or toss and cook the other side.

6. When done, turn upside down onto a plate so that the side first cooked ends up on the outside when the pancake is rolled.

7. To complete the pancake use one of the following fillings and serve immediately.

LEMON PANCAKES

When each pancake is cooked turn it onto a plate sprinkled with raw cane sugar. Brush with lemon juice, roll up, and serve.

HONEY PANCAKES

Spread each pancake with a thin layer of honey, sprinkle with lemon juice, roll up, and serve.

6.

SALADS

Serve a selection of salads to balance your barbecue food and provide more variation and interest to the meal. Try a selection from the following:

TOMATO SALAD

Imperial (Metric)	American
1 lb (455g) firm tomatoes	1 pound firm tomatoes
2 tablespoonsful fresh chopped herbs	2 tablespoonsful fresh chopped herbs
Freshly ground black pepper	Freshly ground black pepper
Olive oil	Olive oil
Sea salt	Sea salt

1. Slice the tomatoes and arrange on a shallow dish.

2. Sprinkle with fresh chopped herbs; basil is best, but parsley, chives, or chervil are good. Season with freshly ground black pepper.

3. When ready to serve, sprinkle with a few drops of olive oil and some sea salt. Don't keep this salad hanging about as the salt soon makes the tomatoes soft and watery.

GREEN SALAD WITH LEMON FRENCH DRESSING

Imperial (Metric)	American
Handful young spinach leaves	Handful young spinach leaves
1 bunch watercress	1 bunch watercress
1 crisp lettuce	1 crisp lettuce
1 chicory heart	1 endive heart
4 nasturtium leaves	4 nasturtium leaves

For the dressing:

Imperial (Metric)	American
3 tablespoonsful salad oil	3 tablespoonsful salad oil
1 tablespoonful lemon juice	1 tablespoonful lemon juice
Sea salt and freshly ground black pepper	Sea salt and freshly ground black pepper

1. Wash all the ingredients and drain or shake dry.

2. Shred the spinach, watercress, lettuce and chicory (endive).

3. Tear the nasturtium leaves into small pieces.

4. Prepare a dressing by shaking the oil, lemon juice and seasoning in a bottle.

5. Toss the salad with the dressing and make sure the ingredients are thoroughly mixed before serving.

CARROT AND ORANGE SALAD

Imperial (Metric)
2 large carrots
Sea salt and freshly ground black
  pepper
Small orange, split into segments
½ tablespoonful olive oil
Juice of 1 orange

American
2 large carrots
Sea salt and freshly ground black
  pepper
Small orange, split into segments
½ tablespoonful olive oil
Juice of 1 orange

1. Grate the carrots finely and season with salt and freshly ground pepper.

2. Mix with the orange segments.

3. Toss with olive oil and the freshly squeezed juice of an orange.

GRATED BEETROOT SALAD

This makes an attractive contrast to the previous salad. Try serving it on a plate surrounded by Carrot and Orange Salad.

Imperial (Metric)
1 medium beetroot, uncooked
Sea salt and freshly ground black
  pepper
⅓ cupful French Dressing

American
1 medium beet, uncooked
Sea salt and freshly ground black
  pepper
⅓ cupful French Dressing

1. Grate the beetroot (beet) finely and season with sea salt and freshly ground pepper.

2. Toss with the dressing and serve.

ONION AND TOMATO SALAD

Imperial (Metric)	American
6 firm tomatoes	6 firm tomatoes
1 small onion	1 small onion
Sea salt	Sea salt
Pinch cayenne pepper	Pinch cayenne pepper
2 teaspoonsful fresh lemon juice	2 teaspoonsful fresh lemon juice

1. Dip the tomatoes in boiling water for a few seconds then peel.

2. Cut into quarters and remove the pips, then slice the remaining flesh into strips.

3. Skin the onion and cut into very thin slices.

4. Mix with the tomato and season with sea salt, cayenne pepper and fresh lemon juice.

MUSHROOM SALAD

Imperial (Metric)	American
½ lb (225g) mushrooms	4 cupsful mushrooms
Juice of 1 lemon	Juice of 1 lemon
4 tablespoonsful olive oil	4 tablespoonsful olive oil
1 clove garlic	1 clove garlic
Handful chopped parsley	Handful chopped parsley
Sea salt and freshly ground black pepper	Sea salt and freshly ground black pepper

1. Choose large fresh buttons and slice vertically without removing the stalks.

2. In a small bowl mix the lemon juice with the olive oil and pulped garlic.

3. Pour this mixture over the mushrooms and sprinkle with chopped parsley, salt and pepper.

BEANSPROUT SALAD

Imperial (Metric)	American
4 sticks celery	4 celery stalks
½ bunch watercress	½ bunch watercress
2 cupsful beansprouts	2½ cupsful beansprouts
6 spring onions	6 scallions
3 tomatoes	3 tomatoes
⅓ cupful French Dressing	⅓ cupful French Dressing

1. Chop the celery into small pieces.

2. Cut up the watercress and mix with the celery and beansprouts in a salad bowl.

3. Chop the spring onions (scallions) into 1-inch (2.5cm) pieces and sprinkle over the top.

4. To complete the salad, decorate with thin slices of tomato.

5. Sprinkle with French Dressing.

SPINACH SALAD

Imperial (Metric)	American
1 lb (455g) raw fresh spinach	1 pound raw fresh spinach
1 small onion	1 small onion
2 large tomatoes	2 large tomatoes
3 fl oz (90ml) olive oil	⅓ cupful olive oil
Juice of 1 lemon	Juice of 1 lemon
1 clove garlic	1 clove garlic
Sea salt and freshly ground black pepper	Sea salt and freshly ground black pepper
2 eggs, hard-boiled	2 eggs, hard-boiled

1. Thoroughly wash the spinach in cold running water.

2. Leave to drain in a salad shaker then, using a sharp knife, shred finely.

3. Thinly slice the onions and tomatoes and mix with the spinach.

4. Make a dressing by mixing the oil, lemon juice, and garlic and season to taste.

5. Pour over the dressing, garnish with slices of hard-boiled egg and serve.

CAULIFLOWER SALAD

Imperial (Metric)
1 small cauliflower
Sea salt and freshly ground black
  pepper
½ cupful Lemon French Dressing
  (page 86)
1 tablespoonful parsley, chopped

American
1 small cauliflower
Sea salt and freshly ground black
  pepper
½ cupful Lemon French Dressing
  (page 86)
1 tablespoonful parsley, chopped

1. Break up the cauliflower into separate florets.

2. Season with salt and pepper and toss in Lemon Dressing (page 86) until completely coated.

3. Garnish with chopped parsley.

POTATO SALAD

Imperial (Metric)	**American**
½ lb (225g) waxy potatoes	1½ cupsful waxy potatoes
Sea salt and freshly ground black pepper	Sea salt and freshly ground black pepper
½ onion	½ onion
1 tablespoonful chopped parsley	1 tablespoonful chopped parsley
½ cupful Mayonnaise	½ cupful Mayonnaise

1. Scrub the potatoes and cook in their skins, preferably by steaming.

2. When completely cool, peel and dice the potatoes.

3. Sprinkle with salt and pepper and a few pieces of very thinly sliced onion and some of the chopped parsley.

4. Pour over the mayonnaise and mix gently so that the potato is coated without being broken up.

5. Garnish with the rest of the chopped parsley and serve.

CUCUMBER AND YOGURT SALAD

Imperial (Metric)	American
1 clove garlic	1 clove garlic
Sea salt	Sea salt
1 tablespoonful white wine vinegar	1 tablespoonful white wine vinegar
1 cucumber	1 cucumber
4 fl oz (120ml) natural yogurt	½ cupful natural yogurt
2 teaspoonsful chopped fresh mint	2 teaspoonsful chopped fresh mint
Freshly ground black pepper	Freshly ground black pepper

1. Thinly slice the garlic and sprinkle with salt.

2. Crush it to a pulp with the back of a spoon then mix with the vinegar and leave for 1 hour.

3. Cut the cucumber into thin slices with a sharp knife and arrange in a dish.

4. Stir the garlic and vinegar into the yogurt and add the mint, but save a little of this for garnishing.

5. Season to taste and pour over the cucumber.

6. Sprinkle over the rest of the mint and chill before serving.

CABBAGE AND APPLE SALAD

Red, white or green cabbage can be used in this recipe, or a mixture.

Imperial (Metric)	American
1 small cabbage	1 small cabbage
2 large apples	2 large apples
Juice of 1 lemon	Juice of 1 lemon
Sea salt and freshly ground black pepper	Sea salt and freshly ground black pepper
1 teaspoonful cumin seeds	1 teaspoonful cumin seeds
2 tablespoonsful salad oil	2 tablespoonsful salad oil
1 tablespoonful chopped chives	1 tablespoonful chopped chives

1. Shred the cabbage finely with a sharp knife.

2. Remove the apple cores but retain the skin.

3. Grate the apple and cover immediately with the lemon juice to prevent browning.

4. Mix the apple and cabbage and season with salt, pepper and cumin seeds and sprinkle with oil.

5. Garnish with chopped chives.

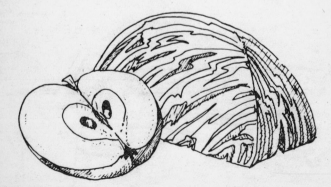

DICED MIXED SALAD

Imperial (Metric)	American
2 sweet apples	2 sweet apples
Juice of 1 lemon	Juice of 1 lemon
½ lb (225g) firm tomatoes	8 ounces firm tomatoes
1 red pepper	1 red pepper
1 green pepper	1 green pepper
3 sticks crisp celery	3 crisp celery stalks
1 onion	1 onion
1 large carrot	1 large carrot
1 tablespoonful olive oil	1 tablespoonful olive oil
½ tablespoonful chopped parsley	½ tablespoonful chopped parsley
½ tablespoonful chopped chives	½ tablespoonful chopped chives

1. Dice the apple into ¼-inch (6mm) cubes and dress straight away with half of the lemon juice.

2. Dice the rest of the ingredients to the same size, and mix together with the rest of the lemon juice and the oil.

3. Decorate with fresh chopped herbs.

RED BEAN SALAD

Any cooked dried bean or cooked fresh broad beans can be used in this recipe. To save time you can use a can of ready cooked beans and many varieties are now available.

Imperial (Metric)
½ Iceberg *or* Webb's lettuce
½ onion
1½ cupsful red kidney beans,
    cooked
Lemon French Dressing (page 86)
Sprig mint

American
½ Iceberg *or* Webb's lettuce
½ onion
1¾ cupsful red kidney beans,
    cooked
Lemon French Dressing (page 86)
Sprig mint

1. Shred the lettuce coarsely and mix with the thinly sliced onion.

2. Add the cooked beans and toss with an oil and lemon juice dressing.

3. Decorate with a few leaves of mint.

MIXED BEAN SALAD

Imperial (Metric)	American
1 cupful aduki beans	1¼ cupsful aduki beans
1 cupful black-eyed beans	1¼ cupsful black-eyed beans
1 cupful vegetable oil	1¼ cupsful vegetable oil
1 onion	1 onion
Olive oil	Olive oil
Sea salt	Sea salt
1 tablespoonful chopped fresh mint	1 tablespoonful chopped fresh mint

1. Start by soaking the beans overnight in twice their own volume of water. As they take about the same time to cook they can be mixed.

2. Cook the beans in the same water for at least an hour until soft but not crumbling apart.

3. Drain thoroughly.

4. Take half the beans and fry them in ½-inch (1cm) of vegetable oil until crisp and browned on the outside.

5. When the fried beans are completely cool mix with the rest and stir in the finely chopped onion.

6. Dress with olive oil and serve sprinkled with sea salt and the chopped mint.

GREEK SALAD

Imperial (Metric)	American
1 large green pepper	1 large green pepper
2 large firm tomatoes	2 large firm tomatoes
1 large onion	1 large onion
2 oz (55g) black olives	½ cupful black olives
4 oz (115g) soft white cheese	½ cupful soft white cheese
2 tablespoonsful olive oil	2 tablespoonsful olive oil
1 tablespoonful white wine vinegar	1 tablespoonful white wine vinegar
or lemon juice	*or* lemon juice

1. In a salad bowl make layers of sliced green pepper, tomatoes, and onion.

2. Add a few olives and top with some soft white cheese (cottage or curd cheese are suitable).

3. Dress with the best olive oil and a little vinegar or lemon juice.

CREAM CHEESE WITH APPLE AND WALNUT SALAD

Imperial (Metric)	**American**
2 sharp eating apples	2 sharp eating apples
Juice of 1 lemon	Juice of 1 lemon
4 oz (115g) cream cheese	½ cupful cream cheese
2 sticks celery	2 celery stalks
1 oz (30g) walnut halves	¼ cupful English walnut halves

1. Core and peel the apples and cut into rings.

2. Dip each ring immediately into a bowl containing lemon juice.

3. Place the cream cheese in the centre of a shallow dish or plate and arrange around it the apple rings, chopped celery and walnut halves.

COLESLAW

Imperial (Metric)	American
1 small white cabbage	1 small white cabbage
1 carrot	1 carrot
1 onion	1 onion
Sea salt and freshly ground black pepper	Sea salt and freshly ground black pepper
½ cupful Mayonnaise	½ cupful Mayonnaise

1. Grate the cabbage and carrot with a coarse grater.

2. Slice the onion very thinly.

3. Season with salt and pepper then stir in the dressing.

Note: To vary use French Dressing. Green or red pickling cabbage can also be substituted, and give interesting visual effect.

RICE SALAD

Imperial (Metric)	**American**
4 spring onions	4 scallions
2 tomatoes	2 tomatoes
2 courgettes	2 zucchini
Bunch radishes	Bunch radishes
2 cupsful cold cooked brown rice (page 72)	2½ cupsful cold cooked brown rice (page 72)
2 tablespoonsful chopped fresh herbs,	2 tablespoonsful chopped fresh herbs
1 cupful Garlic Mayonnaise	1¼ cupful Garlic Mayonnaise
½ teaspoonful sea salt	½ teaspoonful sea salt

1. Chop the spring onions (scallions) and tomatoes and dice the courgettes (zucchini).

2. Remove the leaves from the radishes but leave whole.

3. Mix all the ingredients together in a large bowl, making sure the mayonnaise is well distributed.

RICE AND BEAN SALAD

Imperial (Metric)	American
1 onion	1 onion
½ cucumber	½ cucumber
1 red pepper	1 red pepper
2 oz (55g) black olives	½ cupful black olives
1 cupful cooked beans	1¼ cupsful cooked beans
2 cupsful cooked brown rice (page 72)	2½ cupsful cooked brown rice (page 72)
½ teaspoonful sea salt	½ teaspoonful sea salt
Juice of 1 lemon	Juice of 1 lemon
3 tablespoonsful olive oil	3 tablespoonsful olive oil

1. Chop the onion, cucumber and red pepper into small pieces.

2. Cut the olives in half and remove the stones.

3. Mix with the beans and brown rice in a large bowl.

4. Sprinkle on the sea salt, lemon juice and olive oil and stir well.

7.

SAUCES, RELISHES AND EXTRAS

Simple meals are often the most appreciated and, using some of the following recipes, you can transform very simple barbecue meals into something which seems quite special. The various butters can be used in potatoes, on bread, or for basting. Sauces can be used as a dip or poured over barbecue foods, and relishes add a sparkle to even the dullest meal. Garlic bread is always popular, and is useful for mopping up the sauces, and there are two delicious drinks to complete the meal.

HERB BUTTER

Use in place of ordinary butter with baked potatoes or with any of the recipes in this book where butter is an ingredient. Use whatever herb or selection of herbs you prefer. Try basil, bay, chervil, chives, dill, garlic, marjoram, parsley, rosemary, sage, tarragon, thyme, lemon balm, mint, summer savory, fennel or lovage. If you prefer margarine, use only good quality soft vegetable margarine. Do not use slimmers margarine which has a high water content.

Imperial (Metric)
4 oz (115g) salted butter *or* polyunsaturated vegetable margarine
3 tablespoonsful chopped fresh mixed herbs

American
½ cupful salted butter *or* polyunsaturated vegetable margarine
3 tablespoonsful chopped fresh mixed herbs

1. Cream the softened butter or margarine, with an electric mixer or by hand using a wooden spoon.

2. Stir in the chopped herbs of your choice.

LEMON AND PARSLEY BUTTER

This butter is delicious with baked potatoes or as a baste for kebabs.

Imperial (Metric)
4 oz (115g) salted butter
Juice of 1 lemon
2 tablespoonsful chopped fresh
parsley

American
½ cupful salted butter
Juice of 1 lemon
2 tablespoonsful chopped fresh
parsley

1. Heat the butter over a low heat until melted and beginning to brown a little.

2. Remove from the heat, pour in the lemon juice and add the parsley.

3. Stir thoroughly, and leave to cool.

GARLIC BUTTER

Imperial (Metric)
2 cloves garlic
¼ teaspoonful sea salt
4 oz (115g) salted butter
1 tablespoonful lemon juice
Freshly ground black pepper

American
2 cloves garlic
¼ teaspoonful sea salt
½ cupful salted butter
1 tablespoonful lemon juice
Freshly ground black pepper

1. Thinly slice the garlic with a sharp knife.

2. Place on a saucer, sprinkle with sea salt and crush together with a spoon.

3. In a bowl, cream the butter with a spoon then add the garlic and lemon juice.

4. Mix thoroughly and add freshly ground pepper to taste.

HORSE-RADISH BUTTER

Imperial (Metric)	American
4 oz (115g) soft butter *or* polyunsaturated margarine	½ cupful soft butter *or* polyunsaturated margarine
1 tablespoonful prepared mustard	1 tablespoonful prepared mustard
1 teaspoonful prepared horseradish	1 teaspoonful prepared horseradish
½ teaspoonful sea salt	½ teaspoonful sea salt
Freshly ground black pepper	Freshly ground black pepper
1 tablespoonful chopped parsley	1 tablespoonful chopped parsley

1. Combine all the ingredients except the parsley.

2. Cream until thoroughly mixed and light fluffy texture is achieved.

3. Garnish with chopped parsley and serve with corn on the cob or potatoes baked in their jackets.

ANISEED BUTTER

Imperial (Metric)	American
1 teaspoonful aniseed	1 teaspoonful aniseed
1 teaspoonful boiling water	1 teaspoonful boiling water
4 oz (115g) butter	½ cupful butter

1. Soften the aniseed by pouring over one teaspoonful boiling water and leave to stand for 30 minutes.

2. Add the aniseed and water to the softened butter.

3. Beat with an electric mixer or wooden spoon until fluffy.

TOMATO RELISH

This delicious relish is far better than any bought alternative that I have tasted. It is easy to make and needs no cooking. You will need four 1 lb (500g) jam jars or equivalent.

Imperial (Metric)	American
4 lb (2.3 kilos) ripe tomatoes	4 pounds ripe tomatoes
1½ lb (680g) shallots	1½ pounds shallots
1 oz (30g) sea salt	2 tablespoonsful sea salt
3 large sticks celery	3 large celery stalks
1 red pepper	1 red pepper
1 lb (455g) Demerara sugar	2⅔ cupsful Demerara sugar
1 tablespoonful mustard seeds	1 tablespoonful mustard seeds
¾ pint (425ml) white wine vinegar	2 cupsful white wine vinegar

1. Peel the tomatoes by dipping briefly in boiling water.

2. Chop the tomatoes and shallots finely, sprinkle with the salt and leave overnight, or for at least 8 hours.

3. Place the tomatoes and shallots in a sieve and rinse under cold running water, then leave until well drained.

4. Chop the celery and the de-seeded pepper and mix together in a bowl.

5. Add the sugar, mustard seeds, vinegar, and lastly the tomatoes and shallots.

6. Pot into jars, seal, and keep for at least 6 weeks before using.

SWEETCORN RELISH

This is a relish you can make yourself the day before the barbecue.
Make it as spicy or as mild as you wish.

Imperial (Metric)	American
2 large cooking apples	2 large cooking apples
2 celery sticks	2 celery stalks
1 red pepper	1 red pepper
1 green pepper	1 green pepper
4 spring onions	4 scallions
1 small clove garlic	1 small clove garlic
½ lb (225g) sweetcorn, frozen *or* tinned	1½ cupsful sweetcorn, frozen *or* tinned
2 tablespoonsful brown sauce	2 tablespoonsful brown sauce
¼ teaspoonful sea salt	¼ teaspoonful sea salt

1. Peel and core the apples and place in a saucepan with just enough water to cover the bottom.

2. Heat until the apples become soft.

3. Finely chop the celery, peppers, spring onions (scallions) and garlic.

4. If you are using tinned sweetcorn, drain off the water.

5. Mix all the ingredients together and leave to stand in a covered bowl overnight.

APPLE CHUTNEY

Imperial (Metric)	American
1 large apple	1 large apple
1 medium onion	1 medium onion
3 tomatoes	3 tomatoes
3 sticks celery	3 celery stalks
1 green pepper	1 green pepper
1 clove garlic	1 clove garlic
2 tablespoonsful raw cane sugar	2 tablespoonsful raw cane sugar
2 tablespoonsful cider vinegar	2 tablespoonsful cider vinegar
1 level teaspoonful sea salt	1 level teaspoonful sea salt
Freshly ground black pepper	Freshly ground black pepper

1. Peel and grate the apple and onion.

2. Place the tomatoes in boiling water for a few seconds, remove the skins and chop.

3. Chop the celery and pepper into small pieces.

4. Slice the garlic and crush with a little salt.

5. Mix all the ingredients together in a saucepan and bring to the boil.

6. Simmer over a gentle heat for 10 minutes then remove from the heat.

7. Serve when completely cool.

BARBECUE SAUCE

This is an excellent general purpose barbecue sauce and can be used on burgers, kebabs, potatoes and vegetable dishes. It will keep for up to ten days if refrigerated.

Imperial (Metric)	American
2 oz (55g) butter	¼ cupful butter
1 onion	1 onion
1 clove garlic	1 clove garlic
2 tablespoonsful wine vinegar	2 tablespoonsful wine vinegar
¼ pint (140ml) orange juice	⅔ cupful orange juice
2 teaspoonsful English mustard, ready mixed	2 teaspoonsful English mustard, ready mixed
2 tablespoonsful soft raw cane sugar	2 tablespoonsful soft raw cane sugar
2 slices lemon	2 slices lemon
¼ teaspoonful cayenne pepper	¼ teaspoonful cayenne pepper
6 tablespoonsful tomato purée	6 tablespoonsful tomato paste
Few drops *Tabasco* sauce	Few drops *Tabasco* sauce
Sea salt	Sea salt

1. Melt the butter in a saucepan and gently sauté the thinly sliced onion and pulped garlic for a few minutes, but do not allow to brown.

2. Add the vinegar, orange juice, mustard, sugar and lemon slices, having first removed any pips.

3. Season with cayenne pepper and bring to the boil, then leave to simmer very gently for 20 minutes.

4. Stir in the remaining ingredients and season with *Tabasco* sauce and salt to taste.

5. Allow a further 5 minutes simmering then remove the lemon slices and leave to cool. The flavour is best if left for at least 12 hours before use.

HOT APPLE SAUCE

This sauce is good for hamburgers and hot dogs. It can also be served cold.

Imperial (Metric)	American
1 lb (455g) cooking apples	1 pound cooking apples
1 small onion	1 small onion
2 cloves	2 cloves
¼ teaspoonful ground ginger	¼ teaspoonful ground ginger
Pinch cayenne pepper	Pinch cayenne pepper
4 tablespoonsful white wine vinegar	4 tablespoonsful white wine vinegar
1 oz (30g) soft raw cane sugar	2 tablespoonsful soft raw cane sugar
¼ teaspoonful sea salt	¼ teaspoonful sea salt

1. Peel, core, and chop the apples.

2. Skin and slice the onion and put with the apples, spices and 2 tablespoonsful of vinegar into a pan.

3. Cook over a very low heat until the apples soften, then liquidize or press through a sieve.

4. Return the pulp to the pan, add the remaining vinegar and the sugar and salt and simmer gently for 10 minutes.

5. Serve whilst still hot.

MUSHROOM SAUCE

This hot, tasty sauce is good with sausages, baked potatoes and burgers. It can be cooked beforehand and re-heated very slowly over the barbecue.

Imperial (Metric)	American
1 oz (30g) butter	2½ tablespoonsful butter
1 onion	1 onion
½ lb (225g) large mushrooms	4 cupsful large mushrooms
1 tablespoonful 81 per cent wholemeal flour	1 tablespoonful 81 per cent wholewheat flour
½ pint (285ml) vegetable stock	1⅓ cupsful vegetable stock
1 teaspoonful yeast extract	1 teaspoonful yeast extract
Few drops *Tabasco* sauce	Few drops *Tabasco* sauce
Sea salt and freshly ground black pepper	Sea salt and freshly ground black pepper

1. Melt the butter in a heavy pan and fry the finely chopped onion for a few minutes.

2. Chop the mushrooms into very small pieces and add to the pan, cooking for a few more minutes until the juice begins to run.

3. Turn off the heat and stir in the flour.

4. Cook for 1 minute, then start to add the vegetable stock, little by little, stirring constantly.

5. Add the yeast extract, *Tabasco* sauce and season to taste.

6. Simmer for 10 more minutes, then serve.

GARLIC BREAD

This is delicious served hot with other barbecue bread, and it's very easy to do.

Imperial (Metric)
1 wholemeal French loaf
4 oz (115g) butter *or* polyunsaturated vegetable margarine
2 cloves garlic
Sea salt

American
1 wholewheat French loaf
¼ cupful butter *or* polyunsaturated vegetable margarine
2 cloves garlic
Sea salt

1. Take a sharp knife and split the loaf all the way down one side so that the two halves can be opened apart.

2. Warm the butter or margarine so that it becomes quite soft.

3. Thinly slice the garlic and sprinkle with salt then crush to a pulp with the back of a spoon.

4. Blend the garlic and butter together then spread inside the loaf.

5. Wrap tightly in a double thickness of foil and place on a moderate barbecue for 15-20 minutes, turning occasionally.

6. Unwrap, cut into slices and serve.

GARLIC ROLLS
Follow the instructions above, but use any wholemeal rolls of your choice instead of the French bread. Wrap each roll individually.

HERB BREAD
Follow the above instructions but use only one clove of garlic and add 1 tablespoonful of fresh chopped parsley and ½ tablespoonful fresh chopped thyme.

CHEESE AND ONION ROLLS
Take wholemeal rolls and split in half. Fill with a slice of cheese and a few thin slices of onion. Season with a little salt then seal in foil and heat over the barbecue for 15 to 20 minutes.

MULLED WINE

This warming drink is ideal for a barbecue and keeps out the cold as the evening gets late.

Imperial (Metric)	American
3 cupsful orange juice	3¾ cupsful orange juice
1 cupful water	1¼ cupful water
1 cupful dark raw cane sugar	1¼ cupful dark raw cane sugar
1 cinnamon stick	1 cinnamon stick
4 cloves	4 cloves
¼ teaspoonful freshly grated nutmeg	¼ teaspoonful freshly grated nutmeg
1 lemon	1 lemon
4 bottles red wine, Burgundy or similar	4 bottles red wine, Burgundy or similar
Miniature bottle of French brandy	Miniature bottle of French brandy

1. Take a large saucepan and warm the orange juice, water, sugar and spices in a pan until the sugar dissolves.

2. Add the thinly sliced lemon and leave to stand for 20 minutes.

3. Pour in the wine and heat slowly but do not on any account allow to boil.

4. Keep warm at the edge of the barbecue and serve from the pan with a ladle.

HOT FRUIT PUNCH

Another hot drink for parties and festive occasions.

Imperial (Metric)	American
1 large orange	1 large orange
2 apples	2 apples
6 cloves	6 cloves
2 bottles red wine	2 bottles red wine
2 bottles white wine	2 bottles white wine
2 cupsful orange juice	2½ cupsful orange juice
1 cinnamon stick	1 cinnamon stick
¼ bottle rum	¼ bottle rum

1. Wash the orange then spike with the cloves.

2. Peel the apples and wrap the apple *peel* and the orange in foil and bake for 20 minutes over a moderate barbecue.

3. Pour the wine and orange juice into a large saucepan.

4. Add the roasted orange and the cinnamon stick and warm over the barbecue until the punch begins to steam.

5. Remove from the heat, stir in the rum and serve.

8.

BARBECUED DESSERTS

BAKED APPLES

This easy and much appreciated sweet can be prepared well in advance of the barbecue then placed at the side of the grill to slowly cook while you do the rest of the food. Bramley apples are particularly recommended.

Imperial (Metric)	American
4 large cooking apples	4 large cooking apples
4 oz (115g) sultanas	¾ cupful golden seedless raisins
2 oz (55g) soft raw cane sugar	⅓ cupful soft raw cane sugar
Juice of 1 lemon	Juice of 1 lemon
1 oz (30g) butter	2½ tablespoonsful butter

1. Wash the apples and remove their cores.

2. Place each apple on a double thickness of foil, large enough to wrap it up in.

3. Mix the sugar and sultanas (golden seedless raisins) and pack into the core of each apple.

4. Squeeze a few drops of lemon juice into each core.

5. Top with a knob of butter.

6. Wrap up the apple and join the edges of the foil by folding into a tight seam so that the apple is completely sealed.

7. Place at the edge of the grill where there is a moderate heat and

turn every so often to ensure even cooking, which should take about 45 minutes.

8. Before serving, test one by opening the foil to see if it is soft. If ready, turn into a bowl and serve with double cream.

BANANA SHORTCAKE

Bananas lend themselves particularly well to barbecue cooking being easy to prepare and quick to cook.

Imperial (Metric)	American
2 tablespoonsful butter *or* polyunsaturated vegetable margarine	2 tablespoonsful butter *or* polyunsaturated vegetable margarine
3 ripe bananas	3 ripe bananas
2 tablespoonsful lemon juice	2 tablespoonsful lemon juice
2 oz (55g) dark raw cane sugar *or* honey	⅓ cupful dark raw cane sugar *or* ¼ cupful honey
¼ teaspoonful cinnamon	¼ teaspoonful cinnamon
4 round wholemeal shortbreads	4 round wholewheat shortbreads
¼ pint (140ml) double cream	⅔ cupful heavy cream

1. Melt the butter or margarine in a frying pan over the hot coals.

2. Slice the bananas two or three times lengthways and add to the pan.

3. Sprinkle on the lemon juice and sugar and cook until the bananas become mushy.

4. Meanwhile lightly toast the shortbreads on the grill.

5. Place each shortbread on a plate and serve with a dollop of banana and the syrup from the pan.

6. For an extra luxurious dessert, serve with a spoonful of whipped double cream.

BAKED BANANAS

This very satisfying sweet can be prepared well before the barbecue and bakes over a cool part of the fire in only a few minutes.

Imperial (Metric)	American
4 bananas	4 bananas
4 oz (115g) almonds, blanched	1 cupful almonds, blanched
2 oz (55g) Barbados sugar	1/3 cupful Barbados sugar
1/4 pint (140ml) double cream	2/3 cupful heavy cream

1. Prepare a double thickness of cooking foil, about 1 foot (30cm) square.

2. Place the peeled bananas in the centre of this and sprinkle on the nuts and sugar.

3. Bake for 15 minutes on a cool part of the fire.

4. When cooked, spoon into bowls and top with dollops of cream.

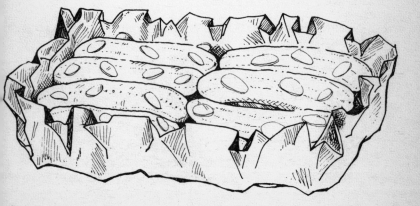

BARBECUED BANANAS

In contrast to the previous recipes this method of cooking bananas is very basic. Although the bananas may look blackened and burnt on the outside, they will be succulent and delicious on the inside.

Imperial (Metric)	American
4 bananas	4 bananas
Juice of 1 lemon	Juice of 1 lemon
Honey or maple syrup	Honey or maple syrup

1. Grill the bananas in their skins over a medium grill for 15 to 20 minutes, turning occasionally.

2. Split open the charred skin to reveal the succulently cooked flesh.

3. Sprinkle with lemon juice and honey or maple syrup and serve in their skins.

PEACH AND PLUM KEBABS

Kebabs have already been mentioned earlier in the book in a savoury context, but many fruits can be successfully barbecued to produce delicious sweets. Only allow sufficient cooking time for the fruit to heat through.

Imperial (Metric)	American
1½ lb (680g) peaches	1½ pounds peaches
1½ lb (680g) plums	1½ pounds plums
3 tablespoonsful honey	3 tablespoonsful honey
Juice and grated peel of 1 orange	Juice and grated peel of 1 orange
2 tablespoonsful water	2 tablespoonsful water
Clotted cream to serve	Clotted cream to serve

1. Cut the fruit into quarters, removing the stones in the process.

2. Mix the honey, orange juice and peel, and the water in a saucepan and warm gently until the honey dissolves.

3. Pour over the fruits in a bowl and leave to cool for an hour or so.

4. Skewer the fruits and cook over a medium heat for 5 to 10 minutes, turning frequently.

5. Serve with some of the honey syrup as a sauce, and a spoonful of fresh clotted cream.

INDEX